Outposts of Hope

OUTPOSTS OF HOPE

—First Peter's Christ for Culture Strategy—

Douglas D. Webster

CASCADE *Books* • Eugene, Oregon

OUTPOSTS OF HOPE
First Peter's Christ for Culture Strategy

Copyright © 2015 Douglas D. Webster. All rights reserved. Except for brief quotations in critical publications or reviews, no part of this book may be reproduced in any manner without prior written permission from the publisher. Write: Permissions. Wipf and Stock Publishers, 199 W. 8th Ave., Suite 3, Eugene, OR 97401.

Cascade Books
An Imprint of Wipf and Stock Publishers
199 W. 8th Ave., Suite 3
Eugene, OR 97401

www.wipfandstock.com

ISBN 13: 978-1-4982-0066-0

Cataloguing-in-Publication Data

Webster, Douglas D.

Outposts of hope : First Peter's Christ for culture strategy / Douglas D. Webster.

vi + 166 p. ; 23 cm. Includes bibliographical references.

ISBN 13: 978-1-4982-0066-0

1. Bible. Peter, 1st—Commentaries. 2. Pastoral theology. I. Title.

BS2795.3 .W36 2015

Manufactured in the U.S.A.   01/05/2015

for

Liam Douglas Webster, Madelyn Allison Webster, Micah Patrick King

resident aliens in a First Peter world

If you fly into Accra, take a small plane to Kamasi, then drive four hours north, you will discover an outpost of hope in a small village called Carpenter. Several times a year pastors from all over northern Ghana gather for worship, fellowship, and study. In the midst of poverty, privations, animism, shamanism, and rising Islamism, these pastors and the congregations they guide are an inspiration and example to me of courageous discipleship. They get it. They are resident aliens in a First Peter world.

Contents

Introduction | 1

1 Chosen Outsiders | 10
2 The New Reality | 23
3 Deep Obedience | 35
4 Living Stones | 51
5 Resident Aliens | 67
6 God's Slaves | 79
7 Mutual Love | 91
8 Christ's Passion Embraced | 102
9 Living God's Way | 116
10 A Christ for Culture Strategy | 128
11 Good Shepherds | 140
12 Humility | 152

Bibliography | 163

Introduction

First Peter is important because it develops the believer's foreign status and strangerhood in fresh ways that Christ's followers have not typically embraced. It critiques post-biblical Christianity in the West and inspires no-fear discipleship in the global church. Peter's focus is not on the badness of culture but on the goodness of the Christian even when confronted by social hostility.

A PARABLE

Toward the end of my senior year at Wheaton College, three friends and I took a two-day canoe trip down the Vermillion River in Illinois. None of us had ever been on the river before and we were using a Girl Scout guidebook to navigate. We thought we had lined up the guidebook with where we started on the river. The first day out the book warned of dangerous rapids, but when we came to rapids they were gentle, nothing to worry about. Then the book warned of a waterfall that we might need to portage around, but it too proved uneventful. The guidebook indicated that the river was especially dangerous around an old factory, but we passed by what we thought was the old factory without incident. By now we were laughing at the Girl Scouts and their wimpy guidebook. We were ridiculing its warnings and mocking its notes of caution. We ended our first day around a campfire thumping our male chests and trashing the Girl Scout guidebook.

The next day we came to a set of rapids that was dangerous, followed by a waterfall steep enough to capsize our canoes, followed by an old factory, where the current and the rocks were so treacherous we had to portage. By now it was clear that we had lined up the guidebook with the wrong section of the river. The Girl Scouts were right after all. What they said was dangerous truly was dangerous. Where the river got serious, the guidebook got serious. We were getting much better advice than we thought we were. Our failure to line up the guidebook with the river was our big mistake.

Most Western believers, myself included, read 1 Peter the way we read the Girl Scout guidebook. It doesn't line up with our experience so we question its relevance. But sooner or later, if we are serious about following Jesus Christ, we will find ourselves in 1 Peter.

LINING UP FIRST PETER

> "The family of believers throughout the world is undergoing the same kind of sufferings." 1 Peter 5:9

Peter's thesis is this: the followers of Jesus Christ are strangers in their own homeland. To be born again into a living hope is to become a foreigner in the land of one's birth. Without moving from one country to another, and without crossing any political or regional boundaries, Christians became resident aliens. The impact of the gospel is theological and sociological. Because of Christ, believers re-enter their home culture as immigrants, foreigners, who for all practical purposes are now strangers without status in their home culture. Christ's followers become exiles without being deported, migrants without migrating, and foreigners without traveling to a foreign country. Believers are resident aliens by virtue of their newfound faith in Christ. First Peter is about the social impact of life in Christ and the inevitable clash with culture than ensues because of the "sheer contrariness" of the good news of Jesus Christ.

Suffering and submission are two of 1 Peter's main themes—two unpopular subjects for most believers, but truly essential for Peter's Christ for culture strategy. He wrote to Christians experiencing cultural pressures and social hostilities foreign to many of us today, not because we live in the "Christian West" or in a "free and democratic society" but because we have abdicated the meaning of biblical discipleship. We suffer little because we stand for less than the first recipients of Peter's letter. The apostle's spiritual direction does not apply to us because we have not applied ourselves to New Testament Christianity. As David Bentley Hart notes, we have obscured the "very real and irreducible element of sheer contrariness" involved in setting apart Christ as Lord. Whether it is read in rural Asia Minor or the American Midwest, the gospel is "essentially subversive of the accustomed

Introduction

orders of human power, preeminence, law, social prudence, religion, and government."[1]

The Danish Christian thinker Søren Kierkegaard believed that there was nothing in the popular Christianity of his day that warranted persecution. Christians were assimilated into the culture so completely that there was no real difference between a Christian and a non-Christian. Everyone was a Christian, because no one was a Christian. The world does not persecute the world when it discovers itself in Christianity. Christians cannot be at home in the world and at the same be "a stranger and a pilgrim in the world."[2]

Kierkegaard lamented that "Christianity marches to a different melody, to the tune of 'Merrily we roll along, roll along, roll along'"— Christianity is enjoyment of life, tranquilized, as neither the Jew nor the pagan was, by the assurance that the thing about eternity is settled, settled precisely in order that we might find pleasure in enjoying this life, as well as any pagan or Jew."[3] We have plenty of pastors, "eminently learned, talented, gifted, humanly well-meaning . . . but not one of them is in the character of the Christianity of the New Testament."[4] Spiritual "swindlers" have taken possession of "the firm 'Jesus Christ' and done a flourishing business under the name of Christianity."[5] "Orthodoxy flourishes in the land, no heresy, no schism, orthodoxy everywhere, the orthodoxy which consists in playing the game of Christianity."[6] Kierkegaard claimed that popular Christianity was all about "twaddle, twattle, patter, smallness, mediocrity." Everyone is "playing at Christianity, transforming everything into mere words."[7]

Post-biblical Christianity is altogether different from the Christianity described in the New Testament. Popular Christianity reflects the spirit of the times, not the Spirit of Christ. It is compatible with and conformed to the prevailing culture, whether it be imperial Rome or capitalistic democracy. This Christless Christianity views the New Testament as an historical curiosity, a cultural artifact, to be read out of religious habit or studied as an intellectual exercise.

1. Hart, "No Enduring City," 46.
2. Kierkegaard, *Attack Upon 'Christendom,'* 42.
3. Ibid., 35.
4. Ibid., 29.
5. Ibid., 117.
6. Ibid., 28.
7. Ibid., 108.

Kierkegaard proposed a way to end the hypocrisy.

> Let us collect all the New Testaments we have, let us bring them to an open square or up to the summit of a mountain, and while we all kneel let one person speak to God thus: "Take this book back again; we humans, such as we are, are not fit to go in for this sort of thing, it only makes us unhappy." . . . This would be an honest and human way of talking—rather different from the disgusting hypocritical priestly fudge about life having no value for us without this priceless blessing which is Christianity.[8]

No one takes the Bible seriously anymore because the world is compatible with popular Christianity. Love is god; not God is love. Past perversions are celebrated as freedoms and tolerance trumps truth. Self-expression is the new sacred and a passion for Christ is comfortably compatible with all other passions. No one discerns the difference between obsession and devotion, fandom and faithfulness, consultants and ministers. Everyone does what is right in their own eyes.

First Peter's major themes, suffering and submission, may be relevant for believers living in North Korea but they may seem remote to believers living in North Dakota. We are no longer socially marginalized or ostracized because our Christianity is in bland conformity to the world. We no longer need to encourage believers to endure persecution because the world finds nothing in our lives to persecute. This makes 1 Peter "virtually irrelevant to the bulk of Western readers," because "too much of it is centered on aspects of Christian existence that are far from most Western Christian experiences: social marginalization and suffering."[9] Instead of questioning popular Christianity's cultural conformity, the assumption is made that our world is much nicer and better than first-century Asia Minor.

In the absence of suffering, one author suggests that 1 Peter offers the Western believer a good theoretical study in suffering so that, "if a life of suffering ever became more typical of Western Christians, we should be better prepared." He adds, "But this seems almost silly. No, we must simply admit that the suffering context of the letter makes it more distant for us than for those of our Christian brothers and sisters who are suffering."[10]

First Peter's relevancy to today's disciple of Christ raises an important question. If the messianic community lived the way Peter expected Christ's

---

8. Ibid., 126.
9. McKnight, *1 Peter*, 35.
10. Ibid.

INTRODUCTION

followers to live, would they experience social ostracism, mockery, and verbal abuse similar to that experienced by the first recipients of Peter's letter? To put the question another way: does the Bible correspond to me or do I correspond to the Bible? If our culture is so compatible with our practice or style of Christianity maybe it is because our Christianity is incompatible with the New Testament. One writer asks,

> After all, what really does an American Christian businessman have to do with suffering when he drives a [luxury] car, has media access to all connections wherever he finds himself (in a car, on a golf course, at home, or at work), takes lush vacations several times a year to exotic places, and buys whatever his heart desires?[11]

What if 1 Peter is foreign to the American Christian businessman, not because the culture is compatible with New Testament Christianity, but because the businessman practices a form of popular Christianity? Suppose his faith is more of a private faith and his Christianity permits conformity to the typical indulgences and practices of the world. Perhaps his colleagues and friends hardly even know he is a Christian. He shares their same passion for sports and entertainment. His ethics are shaped more by professional etiquette than the Bible, and his lifestyle reflects the values and priorities of his non-Christian neighbors. He goes to church a couple of times a month and even tithes his six-figure income, but he spends way more on vacations than missions. The only time he opens his Bible is in church and he doesn't pray very much because that's not his thing. He's inclined to blame God when he doesn't get a promotion or his wife gets cancer. The writer has a point. It would be ironic to call such a person an "elect exile" or a "resident alien" because he is so much at home in his home culture.

The question is this: would our social context be so compatible and welcoming if Christ's followers truly practiced New Testament Christianity? What if the problem of 1 Peter's relevancy lies not with a radically different social context, but with our failure to practice New Testament Christianity? What if your typical Christian businessman, even your typical Christian pastor, simply found the Sermon on the Mount boring and irrelevant? What if your average Christian had little interest in praying the Psalms or understanding the Bible? What if popular Christianity could not find itself in the Bible at all?

---

11. Ibid., 253.

Perhaps we are not just out of step with 1 Peter, we are out of step with the New Testament. If 1 Peter is in sync with the rest of the New Testament, then the lack of any real cultural pushback might mean that we either have a very laid back and receptive culture or we are not very authentic disciples of Christ—or both. Instead of becoming strangers in our home culture for Christ's sake, we have become strangers to the New Testament. We have become like the ad for the Unitarian Universalist church: "Instead of me fitting a religion I found a religion to fit me."

The reason Kierkegaard proposed giving the Bible back to God was because Christians were practicing post-biblical Christianity. He likened the New Testament to "a guidebook to a particular country when everything in that country has been totally changed. Such a guidebook serves no longer the serious purpose of being useful to travelers in that country, but at the most it is worth reading for amusement."[12] Kierkegaard's illustration is worth quoting:

> While one is making the journey easily by railway, one reads in the guidebook, "Here is Woolf's Gullet where one plunges 70,000 fathoms down under the earth"; while one sits and smokes one's cigar in the snug café, one reads in the guidebook, "Here it is a band of robbers has its stronghold, from which it issues to assault the travelers and maltreat them"; here it is, etc. Here it is; that is, here it *was*; for now (it is very amusing to imagine how it was), now there is no Woolf's Gullet but the railway, and no robber band, but a snug café.[13]

Admittedly, the original recipients of 1 Peter inhabited a radically different social context from our own. We do not live under Roman imperial rule. Slave labor is not the driving force of our economy. Women are not under patriarchal domination in our culture as they once were. Society has changed, but what is beyond dispute is that Western culture remains antithetical to God's will and hostile to the Jesus way. The imperial Caesar has been replaced by the imperial self. The American Dream has replaced the Pax Romana. Western capitalism still trades in the bodies and souls of human beings. Culture obsesses over sexual freedom and material indulgence. Idolatry is pervasive. Autonomous individualism is the ideal.

---

12. Kierkegaard, *Attack Upon 'Christendom,'* 111.
13. Ibid.

Introduction

If Christ's followers cannot identify with the social alienation and hostility experienced by 1 Peter's original recipients, perhaps the problem lies with our practice of post-biblical Christianity.

SILAS'S VISIT

It is difficult for modern travelers to appreciate the risks and dangers Silas faced to deliver this letter in person. Silas's round-trip journey over land and sea to these outposts of hope must have been arduous. He set out from Rome ("Babylon"—1 Pet 5:13), and sailed across the Mediterranean Sea through the Corinthian straits. He stopped in Delos before boarding a ship traveling through the Aegean Sea. He had already logged a thousand miles by the time he sailed into the port of what is now Istanbul. He then crossed the Black Sea to Amisus, before beginning his overland circuit from Pontus to Galatia, Cappadocia, Asia, and Bithynia.

Silas was uniquely qualified to provide commentary on Peter's letter. Silas was chosen along with Judas Barsabbas to represent the Jerusalem council to the growing Gentile church (Acts 15:22–34). A gifted encourager and preacher, he accompanied the Apostle Paul on his second missionary journey (Acts 15–18). Silas prayed with Lydia, sang with Paul in jail, and strengthened the believers in Berea. In Paul's letters he is identified by his Latinized name, Silvanus (2 Cor 1:19; 1 Thess 1:1; 2 Thess 1:1). If 1 Peter was written around 65 AD, Silas would have been involved in cross-cultural missions for around thirty years.

From the south shore of the Black Sea to the inland territory of Galatia, Silas offered spiritual direction and counsel to these far-flung outposts scattered throughout Asia Minor. I imagine Silas was accompanied by indigenous co-elders as he made his inland trek from one region to another. In each place, believers gathered to hear Peter's letter read and discussed. Although the letter takes only ten to fifteen minutes to read, I suspect that meeting went on for hours, if not days. Silas brought clarification and application. He may have preached to the gathering and counseled various individuals.

Silas was the first missionary-pastor to interpret 1 Peter. Unlike some modern pastors, who may focus on a few key verses, Silas would have naturally sought to present the whole letter from beginning to end in a thorough and careful exposition of Peter's intended meaning. I don't imagine Silas strayed far from his text and his task. He would have identified the tensions in the text, beginning with the key tension introduced in the greeting. He would have drawn attention to the juxtaposition between the humble identity of "resident aliens" and their Trinity-shaped identity, chosen according to the foreknowledge of God the Father, chosen through the sanctifying work of the Holy Spirit, and chosen because of the obedience and sprinkling of the blood of Jesus Christ.

There is plenty of spiritual direction in First Peter that invites further discussion and clarification, and I am sure Silas "preached" the text with great care. Peter consistently built his case on the Old Testament, invariably drawing on the patriarchs and the prophets, along with the Psalms and Proverbs. He did this in a manner consistent with the essential meaning of the biblical passage, even when he only quoted a line in the passage or alluded to a thought. Silas was undoubtedly asked in these gatherings of "chosen outsiders" to elaborate on these foundational Old Testament passages.

Today, we draw on the work of devoted scholars who have explored every facet of 1 Peter linguistically and theologically. They have thoroughly researched the historical, sociological, and grammatical context. As we attempt to preach and teach 1 Peter we need this vital research, even as we need to read the text prayerfully and meditatively. Silas didn't have excellent commentaries; he had something better. He had original sources. He accompanied the Apostle Paul on his mission trips and colabored with the Apostle Peter. He was preeminently qualified to "preach" 1 Peter to the various outposts of hope that he visited in his journey across modern-day Turkey.

Silas's method of communication was conversational and relational. It is hard to imagine it being any other way, given the rural setting, the intimacy of the gatherings, and the culture of hospitality. His method of teaching was personal and direct, just as ours should be. Silas cultivated the art of holy conversation. He discussed 1 Peter's Christ for culture strategy over countless meals with dear friends. Table fellowship was his pedagogical opportunity. He broke bread with these resident aliens and expanded on Peter's spiritual direction.

Silas's missional pilgrimage undoubtedly instilled the message of First Peter in his soul. I imagine that before he was through he had the letter memorized. He became familiar with the questions asked by earnest inquirers. He acquired skill in answering and applying the message in these various rural settings. He expanded on Peter's exhortation and encouragement,

INTRODUCTION

bringing his heart and mind to the task before him. Silas serves as our pastoral model working behind the scenes to articulate the message of 1 Peter. Like him we seek to draw out its implications for today's outposts of hope.

Silas's example inspires me. If he could engage 1 Peter on his long-distance journey, I can follow in his steps. Recently, I had the privilege of spending three full days with seventy pastors in northern Ghana. We studied 1 Peter for four hours in the morning and then in the afternoons they prayed and discussed the impact of Peter's message on themselves and their congregations in their cultural situation. They in turn would preach through 1 Peter in their churches and discuss its meaning over prayer and table fellowship.

Everything about Silas's mission ought to be an example of how to preach and teach 1 Peter faithfully and effectively. It was not enough for Peter to send the letter. He wanted Silas to deliver the letter in person. This remains God's chosen method of communication. The word of God is accompanied by a servant gifted by the Spirit who seeks to interpret, emphasize, clarify, and apply the message to God's chosen outsiders. It has a proven track record and in this age of telecommunications it still remains the best way for encouraging and exhorting Christians in the true grace of God.

1

Chosen Outsiders

> *Peter, an apostle of Jesus Christ. To elect strangers scattered throughout the provinces of Pontus, Galatia, Cappadocia, Asia and Bithynia, who have been chosen according to the foreknowledge of God the Father, through the sanctifying work of the Holy Spirit, because of the obedience of Jesus Christ and the sprinkling of his blood: Grace and peace be yours in abundance.* 1 Peter 1:1–2

In our age of post-biblical Christianity, 1 Peter waits to be discovered. It is not written in secret code or designed to be obscure, but its message remains hidden. Believers have their reasons for ignoring the book of Revelation with its symbols and images, but 1 Peter is as straightforward as it can be, reflecting the personality and method of its author. The letter and the apostle are dynamic. Peter is immersed in the Great Commission, in the struggle for making disciples from every tribe and people group.

The years Peter spent learning from the Master echo in every verse. His theological and ethical compatibility with the Apostle Paul is significant. Instead of arguing over sources and dependencies, we should marvel at how in sync 1 Peter is with the rest of the New Testament. If the quality of the Greek is a little more literary than we imagine a Galilean fisherman producing after thirty years of interaction with native Greek speaking believers, Silas may deserve some credit. Silas, Peter's esteemed coworker, skilled in communications, was in on the ground floor of the Gentile mission. It would be odd if Silas did not have a hand in the literary and theological composition of 1 Peter.

In the past, when I turned to 1 Peter for a sermon text I pulled out a line like, "Always be prepared to give an answer to everyone who asks you to give the reason for hope you have" (1 Pet 3:15). Or, "Cast all your anxiety on him because he cares for you" (1 Pet 5:7). Sadly, my approach evaded the social impact of the letter and the Spirit-inspired message remained hidden in plain sight. My cultural blinders and homiletical habits conspired against the text. Instead of relying on the wisdom of careful biblical scholars, I constructed my "points" more on what I brought to the text than what was in the text. Human interest anecdotes and illustrations carried the day. I failed to wrestle with what it meant to be a foreigner in my home culture. I overlooked Peter's strategy of vulnerability and submission in a hostile culture. I equated the institutional church with Peter's vivid description of the household of God without challenging the incompatibility of the two realities. Simply put, I missed the essence of 1 Peter. The thrust of my sermons had little to do with the heart of Peter's message. It wasn't until I saw the letter as an integrated whole and felt the poignancy of Peter's christological focus that I began to grasp 1 Peter's impact.

ELECT EXILES

Peter wrote to "exiles scattered to the four winds."[1] *Diaspora* literally means "the scattering of seed." These elect exiles or chosen aliens were dispersed throughout the provinces of Pontus, Galatia, Cappadocia, Asia, and Bithynia. The area encompassed by these five regions is known as the Anatolian peninsula and covers some 300,000 square miles.[2] In Peter's day, the region was predominately rural and divided by natural boundaries—mountains, rivers, lakes, and forests. The diverse topography "helped to perpetuate its economic, political, and cultural heterogeneity down through late antiquity."[3]

Most of the New Testament was written to the followers of Jesus Christ living in cities. First Peter is the exception. Peter wrote his letter to believers living in small villages and rural communities. His "hearers" included farmers, fishermen, miners, homemakers, slaves, carpenters, masons, and cattle herders. His mixed audience of Jews and Gentiles was spread over thousands of miles. "Asia, Bithynia, and Pontus were more completely

---

1. 1 Peter 1:1, *The Message*.
2. Thielman, "First Peter," 569. See Achtemeier, *1 Peter*, 83, and Michaels, *1 Peter*, 4.
3. Elliott, *1 Peter*, 86.

Hellenized, Galatia and especially Cappadocia to a lesser extent. . . . The area enjoyed for the most part competent administration on the part of the Romans during the time 1 Peter was written."[4]

The rural character of 1 Peter's recipients is significant. Peter's message is as intellectually and spiritually challenging as the Apostle Paul's urban letters. There is no hint that Peter scales back the depth of his message because of the demographics. Peter assumes a level of intellectual comprehension and interaction that rivals the most sophisticated New Testament audience. He anticipated the believers' ability and maturity to hold in tension their low position in society with their high calling in Christ. He expected them to discern the difference between cultural conformity and faithful engagement. His spiritual direction is deeply rooted in Old Testament theology and Jesus' kingdom ethic. His theology is consistent with the Apostle Paul's Christology and his cruciform social ethic.[5]

First Peter is the outsider's guide to living the Christian life. Peter wrote to the followers of Christ scattered over five rural Roman provinces. Their newfound faith in Christ literally changed their social standing. They became homeless in their home culture. Because of Christ they were perceived as outsiders, foreigners, and strangers in their home culture. First Peter is about the social impact of the gospel. It is about finding our true home in the household of God. Today, we face the same challenge "to take up, dwell in, and live out" our identity in Christ.[6]

What if all this talk of suffering and trials, submission and humility, vulnerability and patience, only distances the modern Christian from this first-century book? It is not too difficult to see how Peter's emphasis on "strangerhood" might be a turn-off to those who pride themselves on leveraging consumer appeal to make the gospel more attractive. It is easy to see how we might be tempted to write off 1 Peter's "strangeness factor" and conclude that Peter's letter is especially relevant for Christians living in Central Africa or in the Middle East or in China.

What did Peter mean when he referred to Christ's followers as "elect exiles" (1 Pet 1:1; 2:11) and "foreigners" (1 Pet 1:17; 2:11)? New Testament scholars debate the meaning of these terms and struggle with culturally

4. Achtemeier, *1 Peter*, 83.

5. This rural demography has special significance for the churches in northern Ghana. The cultural divide in this West African nation between the more powerful, wealthier urban south and the impoverished and isolated rural north relates to the sociological realities implied in 1 Peter.

6. Harink, *1 and 2 Peter*, 19.

equivalent meanings. Was Peter using these terms in a literal, technical sense, with a specific political meaning, the way we might refer to undocumented immigrants or political refugees? Or was he intending a more metaphoric meaning, employing a cultural term for the social alienation experienced by the followers of Christ?

Most everyone agrees that the recipients of 1 Peter suffered as "strangers in a strange land," but John Elliott goes further and narrowly attributes this strangeness to their social status *prior* to their conversion to Christ. Those designated as foreigners, strangers, and "by-dwellers" were either displaced from their original homeland or strangers temporarily visiting or passing through Asia Minor.[7] "Their different languages, clothing, customs, religious traditions, and foreign roots set these aliens apart and exposed them to suspicion and hostility on the part of the native population . . ."[8] They were strangers and socially ostracized before their conversion to Christ. They were like foreign students visiting the West or political refugees fleeing their home country. It was in this state of social alienation that they became Christians and discovered their new home in the household of God. Elliott argues against a spiritualized reduction of 1 Peter that recasts the letter as a theological message for "'pilgrims and exiles in this world' based on a contrast between present life on earth and a future life in the heavenly home."[9]

Elliott's insistence on a sociological definition of "strangeness" *prior* to Christian conversion has the unintended effect of *spiritualizing* 1 Peter for contemporary believers. If the impact of the New Testament letter is primarily intended for displaced people who come to Christ, its application is narrow. If the letter is focused on social dislocation and discrimination prior to conversion, then Peter's message "must be rearranged dramatically in order to speak to a situation where Christians experience little suffering."[10]

Elliott's interpretation of "resident aliens" places too much stock on a narrow, political definition and not enough on the theological and social impact of people coming to Christ. The case for "resident aliens" and "strangerhood" is best made not on preconversion social status, but on the social upheaval brought about by personal faith in Jesus Christ.[11] It is more

---

7. Elliott, *A Home for the Homeless*, 48.
8. Elliott, *1 Peter*, 94.
9. Elliott, *A Home for the Homeless*, 42.
10. McKnight, *1 Peter*, 32.
11. Dryden, *Theology and Ethics in 1 Peter*, 129.

accurate to say that "social estrangement has its origin in the electing grace of God." Conversion leads to the social divide between the people of God and the unbelieving world. This estrangement "is not simply an unfortunate reality to be coped with, but something to be *fostered*."[12]

The recipients of 1 Peter were not displaced refugees who found Christ during their difficult and disorienting exile in Asia Minor. On the contrary, they were indigenous people, very much at home in their native culture—that is, until they became Christians. By virtue of their newfound faith in Christ they became strangers in their homeland. They didn't need to cross any borders or learn a new language to be considered "foreign" and "strange." They became "resident aliens" without moving or changing their dress or dialect. Conversion to Christ had a dramatic sociological impact. On life's surface everything stayed the same. They lived in the same neighborhoods, kept their old routines, and looked the same in appearance. But now, in Christ, life's meaning, purpose, and hope had radically changed. Their personal faith had public impact, not in a showy or triumphalistic way, but in a quiet revolution of values, commitments, priorities, and fidelities. The overnight change in religious rituals and social customs set them apart, as did their practice of Jesus' Sermon on the Mount ethic. In significant ways they became strangers without status in their home culture.

Should Western believers be envious of this first-century strangerhood? In some sense, yes. Western culture assimilates basic moral and spiritual differences well by writing them off as peculiarly private dispositions. The West takes pride in ideological toleration. This makes it easy for Christ's followers to blend in and get along unnoticed. This is true up to a point, but the believer's foreign status becomes readily apparent in social settings outside the Christian home and household of faith, provided that Christians practice their faith. Some believers may have the idea that what sets them apart is debating abortion or gay rights or the freedom of religion, but as important as these issues are, the apostles emphasized the fruit of the Spirit, the character of the Beatitudes, and the believer's willingness to suffer for the gospel. First Peter is important because it develops the believer's foreign status and strangerhood in fresh ways that we have not typically thought through.

A contemporary application of Peter's social analogy might be to liken Christians to expats (the word comes from the Latin, *ex*, "out of", and *patria*, "country, fatherland"). However, the term *expats* is often used for

---

12. Ibid., 129–30.

professionals or skilled laborers and carries the connotation of status. A closer parallel to Peter's thought might be to compare Christians to migrant workers or legal aliens. Imagine the emotional force of being compared to a Mexican migrant worker in America or a Bangladeshi laborer in India. This sociological comparison underscores the lack of status and standing experienced by Christ's followers.

To be identified as a "Christian" was to be mocked as one of "Christ's lackeys." Conversion meant forsaking familiar rituals and customs and pledging exclusive loyalty to Jesus Christ. Believers no longer shared "in the pantheistic and syncretistic spirit of the times."[13] Coming to Christ meant a real departure in spiritual and sociological terms from their prevailing "home" culture. They no longer felt at home in their homeland. The earth had figuratively shifted under their feet.

First Peter develops an altogether different vision of Jesus Christ than the one popularized in our culture. Jesus is the obedient one whose sacrificial death secures salvation for all those born again into a living hope. Peter's emphasis is on the inheritance to come, the believer's eschatological hope, and the culmination of our salvation when Christ comes again. On this side of eternity he envisions a sacrificial life of holy obedience, rather than the fulfillment of the American dream, personal success, and the material good life.

For several years my parents hosted a group of Chinese university students in our home. They were strangers in a foreign land, coping with western New York winters, learning a new language, and adjusting to foreign foods and customs. Before coming to the Chinese Christian Fellowship group, many of these students had never heard the gospel message. They were Buddhists, Taoists, and atheists, but by the mercy of God many came to Christ and were born again into a living hope. They were homeless in a foreign land but found their new home in the household of God.

Upwards of eighty Chinese students filled our home every Friday night with laughter and prayer. Our neighbors could hear their singing and even their prayers. There was always plenty of good food and lively conversation. The students brought their friends and some of them became Christ-followers.

This outpost of hope was made up of doctoral students in physics, math, chemistry, and engineering. They were culturally engaged and growing in Christ. Some of them fell in love. In some instances, my parents

---

13. Elliott, *Conflict, Community, and Honor*, 21.

became sort of surrogate parents, hosting wedding receptions and providing emotional support. Over time, many graduated and found good jobs and became US citizens. Others returned to their homeland of China or Taiwan or Singapore. Their experience of being foreigners in a strange land prepared them for living for Christ as resident aliens in their native lands.

I was a teenager when my parents opened our home to the Chinese Christian Fellowship. Buffalo had been my home all my life, but in my high school I felt like a foreigner. Somehow the Christian faith set me apart as an oddity to my fellow students. Without trying to be different, I was a stranger in a foreign land. I don't recall verbalizing my faith very often or parading my Christianity around. By nature an introvert, I kept to my schoolwork, played baseball, and was on the yearbook committee. My dad instilled within me a strong reaction to hypocrisy and self-righteousness, so I don't think I came across as "holier than thou," but then again, I didn't laugh at the sex jokes, use profanity, or mock teachers behind their backs.

In tenth grade, my high school English class had a unit on public speaking. We were asked to give a fifteen-minute speech to our classmates on the subject of our choice. Most of these speeches were given to a class of about thirty students. Once a week, however, we met in a large lecture hall that seated several hundred students. Unfortunately, if your name fell on the day class was held in a large lecture hall, you spoke to the combined sections of all the English classes. Getting up in front of people is hard enough, but to do it before a couple hundred of your teenage peers was more of a challenge than I wanted. The speech teacher told us that we could pick whatever subject we wanted to speak on. So after some careful thought I chose my subject: "The Most Important Thing in Life to Me" was my working title.

I remember struggling with this speech, hoping that I could communicate to my peers the importance of Jesus Christ. As you might have guessed, the day came for me to deliver my address and we were in the large lecture hall. After it was all over I felt as relieved as I had felt nervous. Student feedback was positive. All five students who were assigned to grade my speech gave it an A, but the speech teacher gave it a D. She was provoked that I had talked about Christ. In her mind, I had violated an unwritten rule that religion is a private matter, best kept between yourself and God. Students had not found it offensive, even though most of them were not followers of Jesus. But she found it deeply offensive.

My English teacher, a tall, thin German man, handed back my speech and grade report. I looked at five A's and one bold red D, which gave me a C for the speech, since the speech instructor's grade was worth 50 percent. The students rated the style, content, and delivery of the speech positively, while everything the speech teacher said was negative. My English teacher muttered under his breath to me, "I didn't count the D. Your speech was good. You earned an A."

For many Christian young people high school is the first real test of their faith. This is when they realize that they are resident aliens in their home culture. The subtleties of social hostility may be difficult to identify and articulate, but they are deeply felt. For Christian students today "life is far darker, far more violent, far more difficult, and far more tiring than adults, including their parents, realize."[14] The loss of a home culture identity requires significant relational support and nurture. The household of God ought to provide the necessary spiritual and emotional support.

If we become socially ostracized in a hostile culture without the caring support of the biblical community, we end up isolated and alone, stranded in no-man's-land. We are neither at home in the culture nor at home in the body of Christ. First Peter seeks to establish our God-centered identity in the household of God to encourage and strengthen Christ's followers. We need safe relationships and intimate settings to grow in Christ and to offset the loneliness and alienation often felt in a culture that is at odds with the gospel of grace. The household of God must be more than a Sunday morning event that gives attenders an emotional and spiritual lift. Peter envisioned a messianic community that encouraged believers "to abstain from sinful desires" (1 Pet 2:11). The household of God provided an intimate forum for loving one another deeply, rather than a platform for a celebrity pastor.

CHOSEN BY GOD

There is no indication that Peter visited this vast territory in person. Pilgrims from Asia Minor were in Jerusalem for Pentecost and heard Peter's sermon and shared the gospel back home. The letter names no specific believers, identifies no particular congregations. Peter's spiritual direction was intended for a huge region and had widespread application to believers throughout Asia Minor.

14. Clark, *Hurt*, 55.

Peter's credibility and pastoral influence rested in the Spirit of Christ, rather than his personal charisma or in his immediate personal involvement. He assumes an eager reception for his spiritual direction on the basis of their shared identity in the triune God, not on the basis of any special personal attraction or having satisfied any ingratiating terms of endearment.

Peter's salutation juxtaposes a sociological description with a powerful theological identity. The God-centered, Spirit-dependent, Christ-focused character of the recipients of this letter impacts their lives completely and their social situation radically. Their spiritual identity has changed how they see themselves in society and how society perceives them. The social impact is deep and wide, impacting their lives relationally, intellectually, vocationally, politically, and economically. In every way their self-understanding and their perception of the world around them has changed. Now, instead of being defined primarily by their ethnicity or their occupation or their social class they are defined by God.

Implied in this new self-identity is Jesus' description of Beatitude-based believers and Paul's description of the one new humanity. Paul framed the believer's profile positively: "You are no longer foreigners and strangers, but fellow citizens with God's people and also members of his household . . ." (Eph 2:19). In harmony with Paul's description, but from a different perspective, Peter describes the social impact of being Christ's followers and members of God's household. We can debate the English phrasing of Peter's description—"elect exiles," "foreigners," "strangers," "resident aliens"—but in the end Peter is referring to believers as cultural "outsiders." Christians are friendly prophets, Christ's ambassadors, with salt and light impact in a world opposed to God's will and way.

Three phrases in the opening greeting develop a definitive theological identity. Peter's "resident aliens" have been chosen according to the foreknowledge of God the Father, through the sanctifying work of the Spirit, because of the obedience of Jesus Christ and the sprinkling of his blood. This is the theological profile that determines the believer's sociological description. The believers' Trinitarian-shaped identity transcends and subsumes all other regional and tribal identities, but it remains true to the incarnational strategy of the gospel and the reality of the triune God.

The elect exiles are homeless in the hostile hinterland of Asia Minor but at home in the household of God. Christ's followers sing two songs: "This is my Father's world" and "This world is not my home, I'm just a passing through." Paradoxically, believers are simultaneously strangers in a strange land and the beneficiaries of a home-field advantage. They are social outsiders and God's insiders.

Believers are chosen in three ways, with each way embedded in the other two ways. To be chosen according to the foreknowledge of God the Father depends on the sanctifying work of the Spirit and on the obedience and sacrifice of Jesus Christ. Each way stands for the other two. The work of God in conversion is much like the personhood of God within Trinity; it cannot be separated from its roots in the work of the Father, Son, and Holy Spirit, just as the three persons of Trinity cannot be separated from one another. Peter's description is pastoral in nature. He reassures the recipients of his letter that their faith is not the product of their will or wisdom, but the result of God's sovereign initiative and redemptive provision. Peter acknowledges that believers are suffering "grief in all kinds of trials" (1 Pet 1:6). He challenges them to bear up under false accusations (2:12), unjust suffering (2:19), threats (3:13), slanderous ridicule (3:16), and abuse (4:4). The foundation for this challenge rests on their chosenness. They are elected, sanctified, and redeemed by the concerted initiative, effort, and sacrifice of the triune God.

The truth Peter celebrates as the sure foundation for spiritual resilience and social impact is too easily passed over and dismissed by believers impatient with any idea that comes across as a rhetorical abstraction. Serious conceptual thinking and thought-provoking communication faces the danger of being dismissed as "abstract" by believers who are only looking for immediate felt-need satisfaction. Unless meaning is immediately accessible it is in danger of being ignored. Believers who have little patience for the theological foundations of their faith and practice may be risking the integrity and resilience of their faith.

Navy SEALs sometimes suffer from post-traumatic stress disorder, but not at the same rate as regular enlisted soldiers. The lower incidence of PTSD among Navy SEALs is attributed to the extremely demanding Basic Underwater Demolition/SEAL training program. The program is not designed to get SEAL candidates in shape physically as much as it is to get them in shape mentally and emotionally. Of course, recruits have to be in excellent physical condition. But the purpose of the program is to subject recruits to maximum stress in order to test their ability to perform, stay focused, and make the right choices under dangerous and hostile conditions. Researchers have concluded that those who survive the 75 percent dropout rate have learned how to control their emotions in a high-stress environment. They have trained their brain to moderate their emotions so that they can think and act more clearly. Similarly, Christians need theological grounding and training to face life in a sometimes hostile world.

So Peter's salutation is not a religious nicety or a liturgical formula, but the essential truth apart from which we cannot live. Mind-numbing familiarity and listless worship may have more to do with the theft of our God-centered identity than outright social hostility. The intensity of meaning and the true personal significance of being chosen by God is lost by valuing human initiative over divine initiative and self-help strategies over the sanctifying work of the Spirit. If the deep truth of the gospel hits us cold, it may be because we are addicted to giving ourselves the cheap grace that originates in the little trinity of me, myself, and I.

Who is responsible for our narrative? Are we the holy possession of God in Christ, personally chosen by God, predestined for communion with God, adopted into the community of God's people, recipients of God's grace, redeemed by his personal sacrifice on our behalf, and signed, sealed, and delivered by the promised Holy Spirit, *or* are we the accidental product of an impersonal universe, subject to blind chance and random forces, existing in a sphere of energy devoid of promise, plan, purpose, and fulfillment?

With the phrase "sprinkled by his blood" Peter carries his hearers back to Mount Sinai. He links the obedience of Christ and the sacrifice of Christ together. The people of the exodus, after hearing Moses explain the word of the Law, answered Moses, "Everything the Lord has said we will do" (Exod 24:3). Early the next morning Moses built an altar at the foot of the mount. He took the blood of the sacrificial animals and splashed it against the altar and then sprinkled it on the people. He said, "This is the blood of the covenant that the Lord has made with you in accordance with all these words" (Exod 24:8). This solemn act united covenantal obedience and sacrificial redemption in the mind of the people. The sprinkling of the blood reminded the people of the Passover and the instructions given to each family to sprinkle the blood of the Passover lamb on the three sides of the doorframe (Exod 12:5–7).

The image of sprinkled blood is a vivid one. I remember sitting in a crowded New York restaurant with a young lawyer discussing the significance of the Passover and Christ's atoning sacrifice. "Do you know what happens when you take the blood of the lamb and sprinkle it with a hyssop branch against the doorframe?" my lawyer friend asked. In a gesture that caught the attention of others in the restaurant, he jumped up from his seat and swung his imaginary hyssop branch dipped in blood to one side and then to the other and finally straight up and down. "Do you see?" he said. "There in the doorway the sprinkled blood makes the sign of the cross!"

Peter gathers up these exodus remembrances of sacrificial redemption and presents them to the elect exiles for their encouragement and challenge. Our obedience is rooted in Christ's righteousness and atoning sacrifice. We may debate Peter's emphasis: Are we chosen for the purpose of obeying Jesus Christ or are we chosen because of Christ's obedience? In any case, elect exiles are chosen by the foreknowledge of God the Father; they are chosen by the sanctifying work of the Holy Spirit; and they are chosen by Christ's obedience and the sprinkling of his blood.

> To be obedient to Jesus Christ and sprinkled with his blood
>
> *or*
>
> Because of the obedience of Jesus Christ and sprinkled with his blood

The linguistic ambiguity serves to underscore the fullness of the theological truth. We are chosen for a purpose, to obey Christ (objective genitive), and we are chosen because of the obedience of Christ (subjective genitive). Believers place their faith in Jesus and practice the faith of Jesus. Faith and faithfulness cannot be separated. As Bonhoeffer said, "Only he who believes is obedient, and he who is obedient believes."[15] The costly work of the crucified Son inspires the believer's obedience. We have been called to faith and obedience (Rom 1:5).

Peter ends his salutation with a greeting: "Grace and peace be yours in abundance" (1 Pet 1:2). In this simple blessing, the apostle acknowledges the riches of God's unmerited favor and the impact of God's all-encompassing shalom. Everything depends on the Trinitarian-shaped identity—without this theological reality there is no blessing. Bored pew sitters may be tempted to hear it as a throwaway line, a piece of nice-sounding religious rhetoric intoned in clerical professionalism. But it is not an abstraction, it is our life and hope.

Peter summarizes his message in two words: *grace* and *peace*. Everything depends on the grace of Christ. Salvation is by faith alone through grace alone. And God's grace produces peace—peace with God and the peace of God. We are called to be a people of peace, to cultivate inner peace, and to make peace even with those who may despise us, because "God so

---

15. Bonhoeffer, *The Cost of Discipleship*, 69.

loved the world that he gave his one and only Son, that whoever believes in him shall not perish but have eternal life" (John 3:16). In Peter's salutation we hear echoes of Jesus' promise, "I have come that you might have life, and have it to the full" (John 10:10).

John Chrysostom, one of the early church's great preachers, was arrested in Constantinople in 404 because of his faithful preaching. He was deported and exiled to Cucusos, a remote mountainous town in Armenia. In fragile health, he suffered a seventy-day journey lying on a litter pulled by a mule. The trip nearly killed him. Destitute and abandoned, he suffered loneliness and isolation. Everything was taken from him—health, church, friends, ministry, and preaching. Everything but the one thing— the truth that this exhausted fifty-six-year-old prophet-pastor never tired of repeating either in lecture or by letter: his devotion to Christ. "Have you been carried into exile?" John asks. If you are wise, he insists, "you will regard the whole world as a strange country."[16] No one in Christ is at home in this world. We are all chosen outsiders—strangers on earth.[17]

---

16. Chrysostom, "To Prove That No One Can Harm," 274
17. See Ps 119:19.

2

The New Reality

Praise be to the God and Father of our Lord Jesus Christ!

In his great mercy he has given us new birth into a living hope through the resurrection of Jesus Christ from the dead, and into an inheritance that can never perish, spoil, or fade. This inheritance is kept in heaven for you, who through faith are shielded by God's power, and until the coming salvation that is ready to be revealed in the last time.

In all this you greatly rejoice, though now for a little while you may have to suffer grief in all kinds of trials. These have come so that your faith—of greater worth than gold, which perishes even though refined by fire—may be proved genuine and result in praise, glory and honor when Jesus Christ is revealed.

Though you have not seen him, you love him; and even though you do not see him, you love him; and even though you do not see him now, you believe in him and are filled with an inexpressible and glorious joy, for you are receiving the end result of your faith, the salvation of your souls.

Concerning this salvation, the prophets, who spoke of the grace that was to come to you, searched intently and with the greatest care, trying to find out the time and circumstances to which the Spirit of Christ in them was pointing when he predicted the sufferings of Christ and the glories that would follow. It was revealed to them that they were not serving themselves but you, when they spoke of the things that have now been told you by those who have preached the gospel to you by the Holy Spirit sent from heaven. Even angels long to look into these things. 1 Peter 1:3–12

Outposts of Hope

If the message of 1 Peter lies hidden in plain sight, it is not because Christians wilfully ignore Peter's spiritual direction. They don't know it exists. They may read it for devotions or hear it preached in a sermon, but it is easily transposed by our church culture and private piety into innocuous rhetoric. When the biblical text is spiritualized and sermonized Peter's Spirit-inspired exhortation to strangerhood is rendered irrelevant.

ALIEN ALIENATION AND PROGRESSIVE CONFORMITY

First Peter describes a narrow and vital way between two broad extremes. Both extremes represent popular Christianity. At one extreme Christendom is a grassroots civil religion that is antithetical to 1 Peter's cruciform strategy of submission and sacrifice. This version identifies more with the American good life than with Jesus and his Sermon on the Mount. It believes in American exceptionalism and is fiercely loyal to free-market capitalism. Its proponents feel threatened by the "secular" culture and feel compelled to vent their anger against liberals who they believe are destroying America. Their resentment and fear run deep. "Bible-believing" Christians blame the president and his party for the nation's moral degeneracy and economic failings, but what is particularly pernicious is their slanderous disdain and even their wish for his demise. For a generation of professing Christians their hate is deep-seated. They wrap the cross in the American flag and cherish the American Dream as their one great hope, a hope worth fighting for with the weapons of the world.

The other extreme form of Christendom celebrates conformity to the spirit of the times. This "liberal" version of Christendom identifies with "progressive" causes such as gay rights, abortion on demand, and radical pluralism. It is knowingly at odds with the New Testament and 1 Peter's cruciform strategy. Progressive Christendom prides itself on being open-minded and tolerant. It freely diminishes biblical authority on virtually all matters that run counter to the prevailing cultural ethos. Not long ago I was invited to the home of a denominational church leader for the purpose of meeting his gay partner. I went out of respect with the expectation of engaging in a thoughtful conversation. I wanted to understand how this denominational executive related his sexuality to his professed faith in Christ. Sitting across from his gay partner after discussing his expertise in writing computer code, I asked, "How do the two of you discuss the faith?" He looked at me like he didn't understand the question. So, I repeated it, saying, "You know, how do you talk about the Christian faith?" He answered, "Oh, we never talk about the faith. I'm not a Christian. I'm not a believer." The casual confession of unbelief fits this progressive version of cultural Christianity. To deny that Jesus is the Christ was really no big deal for the gay partner of a prominent church leader, nor did the violation of biblical sexual ethics bother the church leader.

Neither form of popular cultural Christianity can identify with the Apostle Peter's description of the "resident alien." The alienation fostered by the "conservative" and "progressive" extremes of Christendom is radically different from the social alienation addressed by the Apostle Peter. Both the "Right's" alienation and the "Left's" progressive conformity are induced by the world. Professing Christians are persuaded to ignore the New Testament and neither extreme practices 1 Peter's Christ for culture strategy. Discerning the difference between cultural conformity and true alienation is critical to understanding the message of 1 Peter.

Peter encouraged the "elect exiles" to embrace with joy the new reality chosen for them by the triune God. They are given new birth into a "living hope," into "an inheritance that can never perish, spoil, or fade." They live into a new reality that far outweighs the social reality of being resident aliens. They eagerly await "the coming salvation that is ready to be revealed in the last time." Instead of suffering deep resentment because of their self-induced ideological alienation, Peter's chosen outsiders are "filled with an inexpressible and glorious joy."

DOXOLOGY

Doxology is the place to begin. *Eulogy* is the key word. Our English word *eulogy* is derived from the Greek word εὐλογέω, which means to speak well of someone, to commend the character and services of a person. We associate the word with praise for one who has recently died, but Peter linked the word to everything praiseworthy of God. As Paul put it, "Blessed is the God and Father of our Lord Jesus Christ" (2 Cor 1:3; Eph 1:3).

Worship in the name of God the Father, Son, and Holy Spirit is the gateway into Peter's theology. There is no nameless generic deity prior to the triune God. Almighty God has willed Godself to be known in person through his revelation, redemption, and sanctification. "Those who conceive of God in His naked majesty apart from Christ," Calvin insisted, "have an idol instead of the true God."[1]

Words—religious words—can drain the energy out of worship. But words full of truth and grace invigorate the soul. Peter's doxology is grounded on bedrock. What follows is built on granite truth. His doxology is *creational*, calling forth a new way of being and living in the world, *constitutional*, celebrating a whole new way of relating to the world, and *creedal*, confessing a new way, rejoicing and hoping in the world. Peter leads us in doxology.

His Trinitarian *inclusio* encompasses his praise, beginning with God the Father and the Lord Jesus Christ and ending with the Holy Spirit preaching the gospel (1 Pet 1:3–12). Similar in pattern to the Apostle Paul's opening benediction in Ephesians, Peter emphasized that it is not what we have done or what we should do, but what the triune God has done that establishes our devotion to God.

Peter's doxology encompasses the scope of salvation from the "new birth into a living hope" to "the end result of your faith, the salvation of your souls" (1 Pet 1:3, 9). In one sentence in the Greek, Peter captures the Alpha and the Omega of salvation, followed by the long-awaited prophetic anticipation of Christ and the cross (1 Pet 1:3–9). Peter celebrates the work of the prophets and the progressive revelation of the gospel of Christ (1 Pet 1:10–12). In the middle of both sections, suffering is a key theme:

> In all this you greatly rejoice, though now for a little while you suffer grief in all kinds of trials (1 Pet 1:6).

> The prophets . . . [tried] to find out the time and circumstances to which the Spirit of Christ in them was pointing when he predicted the suffering of Christ and the glories that would follow (1 Pet 1:10–11).

This doxological introduction is not a rhetorical formality. Peter is not satisfying a liturgical protocol before turning to the real issues. His spiritual direction begins here, in worship of who God is and what God has done. The only way cultural hostility, political harassment, economic discrimination, and relational tensions can be dealt with redemptively is out of a God-centered, cruciform perspective. Before Peter addresses the problem of innocent and unjust suffering, before he offers a spiritual strategy for cultural engagement, he lays out a theological foundation of praise.

---

1. Calvin, *Hebrews and 1 and 2 Peter*, 231.

Peter's approach to pastoral care is worth emulating today. The mercy (ἔλεος) of God brackets this section (1 Pet 1:3—2:10) and draws on Old Testament roots for its meaning. This is God's *hesed* love, his covenant love, his gracious mercy, his loving-kindness (Exod 20:6; Deut 5:10). Mercy is rooted in the character of God and finds its ultimate expression in the merciful act of Christ's sacrificial death on our behalf. We begin here with Peter's Christ for culture strategy.

NEW BIRTH

Peter praises God the Father for giving us new birth into a living hope. Although the particular word Peter used for new birth is unique, the metaphor recalls Jesus' conversation with Nicodemus: "Very truly I tell you, no one can see the kingdom of God unless they are born again" (John 3:3). Jesus' reference to the new birth was not the first time this wonderful image was used in salvation history. Isaiah prophesied the unheard-of good news of a laborless childbirth: "Before she goes into labor, she gives birth.... Yet no sooner is Zion in labor that she gives birth to her children" (Isa 66:7, 8). Ezekiel prophesied new life in the valley of dry bones: "This is what the Sovereign Lord says to these bones: I will make breath enter you, and you will come to life" (Ezek 37:5).

The most far-reaching prophecy of the new birth metaphor comes in Psalm 87. The gates of the city of God are swung open and every nationality finds its new home in Zion. "Indeed, of Zion it will be said, 'This one and that one were born in her, and the Most High himself will establish her.' The Lord will write in the register of the peoples: 'This one was born in Zion'" (Ps 87:4–6). In spite of this rich prophetic background, Nicodemus missed the meaning of the metaphor. "'How can anyone be born when they are old?' he asked. 'Surely they cannot enter a second time into their mother's womb to be born!'" (John 3:4).

The metaphor of birth underscores the fact that this new genesis is not of our own making. We cannot produce this new birth on our own any more than we can be reborn physically. New Testament scholar F. Dale Bruner describes the truth that lies behind Peter's choice of metaphors:

> The genesis of Jesus (and of faith in Jesus) inside any human life ... is the work of the Holy Spirit, the *Creator Spiritus*, who began the world's *creation* ("the Spirit of God swept over the face of the waters," Gen 1:2), and who now begins the world's *new creation*

and its definitive salvation. The permanent value of the creedal doctrine of the Spirit's conception of Jesus in the virgin Mary is this: it is the Holy Spirit *and not human initiative* that brings Jesus into personal life (then Mary's, now ours). When Jesus Christ comes to anyone in history, even in his Advent coming to Mary, it is always the work of the Spirit, not of human preparation or enterprise. *Every conversion is a virgin birth.* "With human beings this [new life] is impossible; but with God absolutely everything is possible" (Matt 19:26). The Holy Spirit, in other words, is the miraculous *how* of New Life."[2]

How do any of us ever come to faith and trust in Jesus Christ? We all are the least likely candidates for conversion. All of us need a miracle to believe. The Apostle John wrote, "Yet to all who received him, to those who believed in his name, he gave the right to become children of God—children born not of natural descent, nor of human decision or a husband's will, but born of God" (John 1:12–13). At a recent anniversary celebration for a church in our city, a visiting local rabbi chided the host pastor with a smile, "You know the difference between us is that you win souls and we make souls." The rabbi's off-the-cuff distinction hit the theological nail on the head. Faith in Christ rests on what Christ makes of us, not what we make of ourselves. Whatever confidence we might have in personal achievement, family heritage, ethnic identity, and religious zeal counts for nothing (Phil 3:7–8).

Peter praises God for giving "us new birth into a living hope through the resurrection of Jesus Christ from the dead" (1 Pet 1:3). Echoes of Peter's Pentecost sermon can be heard in this line with its emphasis on the resurrection of Jesus Christ. Peter delivered the first Easter message before a massive crowd in Jerusalem which included Jewish pilgrims from Cappadocia, Pontus, and Asia (Acts 2:9). Undoubtedly some of the recipients of Peter's letter heard the gospel for the first time at Pentecost and these words brought back vivid memories of their conversion to Christ. Peter chose to begin his spiritual direction with a reminder of their new birth, the foundation for sustained faithfulness and a lively hope.

---

2. Bruner, *The Gospel of John*, 24.

The New Reality

A LIVING HOPE

Peter's opening doxology gives believers three reasons to live for Christ in a difficult culture. We have a *living hope*, a *lasting inheritance*, and a *coming salvation*. We are encouraged to live into this new reality with confidence and joy. Peter did not envision a beleaguered and fearful minority fighting for its life. He saw the chosen outsiders, members of God's household, as the concrete expression of the love and power of God in the world.

The benediction moves from the believer's "new birth into a living hope" to "an inheritance that can never perish, spoil, or fade" (1 Pet 1:3-4). The arduous journey from the new birth to the heavenly inheritance is the focus of Peter's challenging letter. Life in the conflicted middle, between the already and the not yet, is his major concern. He frames the Christian life between two bedrock realities: new birth and the salvation of our souls. Peter praises God for giving new birth to the people of God, and for shielding them "until the coming of the salvation that is ready to be revealed in the last time" (1 Pet 1:5). He links the beginning of the Christian life with the end, in order to demonstrate that faithfulness to the end affirms faith from the beginning. "Today we emphasize the New Birth," writes Peter Gillquist, "[while] the ancients emphasized being faithful to the end. We moderns talk of wholeness and purposeful living; they spoke of the glories of the eternal kingdom. . . . The emphasis in our attention has shifted from the completing of the Christian life to the beginning of it."[3]

Peter expects believers to live through the present trials in the light of their future destiny. Their immediate priorities and life practices are based on a living hope in an inheritance "that can never perish, spoil, or fade" (1 Pet 1:4). Peter alliterated three words in the Greek to modify inheritance (ἄφθαρτον, ἀμίαντον, ἀμάραντον). Christ's followers have an inheritance that is imperishable, undefiled, and unfading. This inheritance fulfills and transcends the covenant promises given to Israel. It is no longer tied to the land or to political autonomy. "The notion of a holy land is superseded by that of a holy community" (1 Pet 2:4-10).[4] This is the inheritance Jesus promised when he said:

> Truly I tell you, no one who has left home or brothers or sisters or mother or father or children or fields for me and the gospel will fail to receive a hundred times as much in this present age:

---

3. Gillquist, "A Marathon We Are Meant to Win," 22.
4. Elliott, *1 Peter*, 336.

homes, brothers, sisters, mothers, children and fields—along with persecutions—and in the age to come eternal life. But many who are first will be last, and the last first (Mark 10:29–31).

When we concentrate on material comforts and physical pleasures, a vivid sense of this living hope and lasting inheritance wanes. In an effort to get more of what the world has to offer, we come up with less. "Our Lord finds our desires not too strong, but too weak," C. S. Lewis chided. "We are halfhearted creatures, fooling about with drink and sex and ambition when infinite joy is offered us, like an ignorant child who wants to go on making mud pies in a slum because he cannot imagine what is meant by the offer of a holiday at the sea. We are far too easily pleased."[5]

Believers in northern Ghana may grasp this challenge more readily than many Western believers. Their hardscrabble existence knows the harsh realities of poverty and disease, whereas we have grown accustomed to expert medical attention and on-demand emergency care. Sadly, it often takes the death of a loved one or a cancer diagnosis for Western believers to see their fixation with material comforts and physical health. Believers living in rural Africa may have a better sense of the inheritance they have in Christ than believers living in centers of worldly power.

Personal ambition can overshadow the divine inheritance and the quest for success can rob the significance of "an inheritance that can never perish, spoil, or fade" (1 Pet 1:4). Our concerns have more to do with retirement, health care, and pensions than with our heavenly inheritance. We work hard to shield ourselves from the vicissitudes and vulnerabilities of life. We are more focused on insurance premiums and our 401(k)s than on being "shielded by God's power until the coming of the salvation that is ready to be revealed in the last time" (1 Pet 1:5).

Dan Lam was a successful businessman headquartered in London, working on construction projects on three continents, supervising 1,500 employees. He came to Christ as a boy in his native Hong Kong. His father died when he was young and Dan was raised by his mother, whose strength and devotion marked his life. He grew up poor, determined to work hard and be a success. Now, in his prime, Dan was a global contractor living in London. Along with his wife, Grace, he attended a weekend retreat on kingdom values hosted by the late John Stott, who was the pastor of All Soul's Church in London. As Grace would later say, that "fateful" seminar turned Dan's world upside down. He became convicted about his need to be better

---

5. Lewis, *The Weight of Glory*, 4–5.

invested in the kingdom of God. He realized in a fresh way that the gospel of hope not only converts the soul but transforms all of life. He remained an active businessman, but his focus became different. He wanted to use his time, energy, and resources to further the kingdom of Christ. Business success became the mere means to that end. Money lost its priority.

Dan was a visionary with a passion for Christ. He was committed to proclaiming the gospel among the unreached. He was a confident, single-minded individual with a mission. The Holy Spirit sanctified his entrepreneurial spirit, making him a gentle crusader, a tentmaker missionary. He could put a peasant farmer in Burma at ease and be every bit the equal to a high roller in Hong Kong. Because of Christ's work through Dan, there are hundreds of Vietnamese pastors preaching the gospel, scores of Cambodian believers are studying the Bible, Mongolians are being taught theology and prepared for missionary service, and Russians in Siberia are growing in their faith.

Dan was restless for the sake of the kingdom. His nonstop networking, facilitating, and empowering impacted indigenous pastors in Southeast Asia, new believers in Mongolia, and North American seminary professors like myself. For years Dan was an ambassador for Christ engaging in global shuttle diplomacy for the kingdom of Christ. On March 22, 1994, Aeroflot flight 593, carrying Dan on a flight from Moscow to Hong Kong, crashed in Russia. All seventy-five people onboard were killed. Believers around the world mourned the loss of a true ambassador for Christ, who invested in the inheritance that can never perish, spoil, or fade.

SALVATION

We have been given new birth into a living hope and a lasting inheritance that cannot be taken away. Peter turns next to "the coming of the salvation that is ready to be revealed in the last time" (1 Pet 1:5). He says four things about this salvation.

Peter's description of salvation is eschatological. He refers to the ultimate deliverance that is to be revealed in the last time. God preserves and protects all those who have placed their faith and trust in him.

Second, salvation is experienced by a faith tested by all kinds of trials. Suffering proves the genuineness of trust in God and results in "praise, glory and honor when Jesus Christ is revealed" (1 Pet 1:7). Peter has much more to say about suffering as a refiner's fire and the role it plays in the Christian's life.

Third, salvation is received by faith, not sight. There is a double stress on the fact that their faith does not rest on their own firsthand, eyewitness experience.[6] Faith is the earnest expectation of sight, but on this side of eternity it is based not on sight but trust.

Fourth, the salvation anticipated by the Old Testament prophets belongs to all who receive by faith the gospel preached by the Holy Spirit. Peter's interpretation of the Old Testament centers on Jesus Christ. Christ is the revelational key for opening up the meaning of the messianic prophecies. Peter simply followed his Lord's hermeneutic, well illustrated in Jesus' conversation on the road to Emmaus: "And beginning with Moses and all the Prophets, he explained to them what was said in all the Scriptures concerning himself" (Luke 24:27). It must have been a wonderful experience to hear Jesus explain "all the Scriptures concerning himself."

We assume that Peter heard these two Emmaus-bound disciples rehearse Jesus' conversation. We expect that Jesus told them about Abel's sacrificial lamb and Abraham at the altar with Isaac, as well as Job's cry, "I know that my Redeemer lives and that in the end he will stand on the earth and after my skin has been destroyed yet in my flesh I will see him" (Job 19:26). Jesus would have spoken of Israel's Passover lamb and Moses raising the serpent in the wilderness. He would have quoted David's prayer, "My God, my God, why have you forsaken me?" (Ps 22:1) and Isaiah's picture of the suffering servant. He would have recalled Daniel's vision of the victorious Son of Man, and Zechariah's unappreciated shepherd and mourned martyr. Luke's description, "And beginning with Moses and all the Prophets" encompasses the whole salvation story from Genesis to Malachi.

Peter reminds Jews from Jerusalem and pagan Gentiles from Pontus that now in Christ they have an ancient heritage to live into. To be chosen by the foreknowledge of God the Father, through the sanctifying work of the Holy Spirit, because of the obedience of Jesus Christ and the sprinkling of his bloo means that their identity and heritage are firmly rooted in a long-standing tradition of salvation. Everybody has a story but only one story redeems our story. Rural farmers in Ghana and middle-class suburbanites in America embrace the same heritage. The believer's freedom and self-identity are no long rooted in ancient rituals and taboos or grounded in national pride and patriotism.

---

6. Elliott, *1 Peter*, 342.

The New Reality

When I first went to northern Ghana to train pastors, I was overwhelmed by the poverty and the hardship of ordinary life in the villages. I was blinded to the depth of character and the spiritual gifts of my brothers and sisters in Christ because of their poverty. I saw them primarily in their need, but now, after repeated visits, I see them primarily as coworkers in Christ. Great strides have been made in providing sustainable social development, but they are still very poor by Western standards. However, now I look past the poverty and see real men and women of God, who have inestimable value in Christ's eyes and in the economy of the kingdom of God.

The centrality of salvation is the cardinal doctrine of the Christian faith. Scot McKnight warns that sincere believers can be "easily led off the track of leading people to salvation" by striving to improve social conditions. He commends humanitarian efforts, but he warns that "social services are never a substitute for the process of salvation." McKnight continues, "When Christians get out of balance here, it is always the message of salvation that gets lost."[7] Salvation is the central reality from which all else flows. To use his metaphor, it is the hub of the wheel and the spokes are the various ministries inspired by and centered in the holistic salvation provided by Christ.

Within this compact and concise benediction Peter lays out the beauty and depth of our salvation. He presents faith as protected by God, tested by suffering, expectant of sight, and grounded in revelation. This faith is worked out in holistic faithfulness to God, meaning that there is true loyalty to God's will and obedience to God's word. The stress is not on faith's feelings and emotions, but on submitting to the rule of faith and the will of God. Peter's focus is on the believer's behavioral demonstration of faith. Faith in Christ means a working, serving, loving, sacrificial faith that belongs to those who have placed their trust and loyalty in Christ.[8]

Like an artist drawing a quick sketch, Peter draws out the meaning of salvation against the backdrop of *eschatology* ("the salvation that is to be ready to be revealed in the last time," 1 Pet 1:5), *suffering* ("you may have had to suffer grief in all kinds of trials," 1 Pet 1:6), and *salvation history*

---

7. McKnight, *1 Peter*, 81.

8. Elliot argues that faith "is the social, externally manifest behavior of loyalty and commitment to another person or group or deity. This contrasts to its meaning in modern society, where attention focuses on individuals and their internal or psychological states of being and where 'faith' or 'belief' usually means individual cognitive and affective assent of mind to truth or teaching. . . . The later concept of 'faith' as a body of transmitted beliefs, the 'faith which is believed' (1 Tim 3:9; 5:8; 2 Tim 4:7; Titus 1:13; 2 Per 1:1; Jude 3, 20; Rev 2:13), does not occur in 1 Peter." Elliott, *1 Peter*, 340.

("the prophets, who spoke of the grace that was to come to you, searched intently and with the greatest care...," 1 Pet 1:10). Salvation is at the core of everything Peter has to say to these chosen outsiders scattered throughout Asia Minor. His theological benediction was meant to change outlooks and transform character.

INEXPRESSIBLE JOY

Living into salvation redefines the disciple's life in every way. In a word, salvation comprehends all that we have been given in Christ. We are saved from "sin and death; guilt and estrangement; ignorance of truth; bondage to habit and vice; fear of demons, of death, of life, of God, of hell; despair of self; alienation from others; pressures of the world; a meaningless life."[9] We are saved for a purpose: to love God, others, and ourselves. We are saved for freedom, mission, and community.

Salvation changes our relationship with God, giving us acceptance with God, forgiveness, reconciliation, sonship, reception of the Spirit, and everlasting life. Salvation changes us emotionally, giving us confidence, peace, courage, hopefulness, and joy. Salvation changes us spiritually, giving us prayer, guidance, discipline, dedication, and service. Salvation changes us personally, giving us new thoughts, convictions, horizons, motives, satisfactions, and self-fulfillment. Salvation changes us socially, giving us a new community in Christ, a compassion for others, and an "overriding impulse to love as Jesus has loved."[10] Living into this new reality makes anger and resentment, no matter how bad the culture is, impossible. Inexpressible and glorious joy is the mark of the Christian. "Even angels long to look into these things" (1 Pet 1:12).

---

9. White, "Salvation," 968. (This entire section on salvation is dependent on R. E. O. White's article.)

10. Ibid.

3

Deep Obedience

Therefore, girding up the loins of your mind, being sober and alert, set your hope fully on the grace that is coming to you at the revelation of Jesus Christ.

As children of obedience do not be conformed to the passions of your former ignorance. But as he who called you is holy, be holy yourselves in all your conduct; for it is written: "Be holy, because I am holy."

Since you call on a Father who judges each person's work impartially, live out your time as foreigners here in reverent fear. For you know that it was not with perishable things such as silver or gold that you were redeemed from the empty way of life handed down to you from your ancestors, but with the precious blood of Christ, a lamb without blemish or defect. He was chosen before the creation of the world, but was revealed in these last times for your sake. Through him you believe in God, who raised him from the dead and glorified him, and so your faith and hope are in God.

Now that you have purified your souls by your obedience to the truth for a sincere love for each other, love one another deeply from the heart. For you have been born again, not of perishable seed, but of imperishable, through the living and enduring word of God. For, "All people are like grass and all their glory is like the flowers of the field; the grass withers and the flowers fall, but the word of the Lord endures forever." And this is the word that was preached to you.

Therefore, rid yourselves of all malice and all deceit, hypocrisy, envy, and slander of every kind. Like newborn babies, crave pure spiritual milk, so that by it you may grow up in your salvation, now that you have tasted that the Lord is good. 1 Peter 1:13–2:3

First Peter's opening greeting and benediction focus attention on the identity of the believer. Peter portrays a whole new personal and social reality for the follower of Christ. God's chosen outsiders have been given new birth into a living hope, into a lasting inheritance, and into a coming salvation. This declaration is followed by an exhortation. Theology is inseparable from ethics. "Therefore" signals a compelling reason for what is to follow. Hope in the coming salvation calls for a life of obedience. Staccato imperatives punctuate Peter's spiritual direction: "Do not conform to the evil desires you had when you lived in ignorance" (1 Pet 1:14); "Be holy in all you do" (1 Pet 1:15); "Live out your time as foreigners here in reverent fear" (1 Pet 1:17). These imperatives set forth an agenda for Christians that is clear and compelling.

NEW MEMBERS

In many churches the threshold for membership is low and new members' classes concentrate more on the basic tenets of the faith than on what it means to be faithful. New members are encouraged to attend church and give generously, but Peter's exhortation opens up a whole new "lesson plan" for new, as well as old, members of the household of God. How we should live is just as important as what we believe.

Peter continued to work his theme of new birth (1 Pet 1:3) with his references to "obedient children" (1 Pet 1:14), "being born again" (1 Pet 1:23), and "newborn babies" (1 Pet 2:2). He begins and ends this section with images that invoke the deeply personal life transformation found in Christ. Peter plays these themes out with rhythm and grace. "Hope" is used three times in this rhythmic pattern: "new birth into a living hope" (1 Pet 1:3); "set your hope on the grace to be brought to you" (1 Pet 1:13); and "your faith and hope are in God" (1 Pet 1:21). His series of negative and positive tensions build until you can almost hear the hungry baby crying for her mother's milk. If you have ever been around a newborn baby who is past her feeding time you know that cry.

In Peter's analogy this is the real hunger that is driven by rejecting the old evil desires that belong to the past and embracing a life of holiness. This is the longing for God that is inspired by the confidence that God's judgment is eminent, just, and fair, and that our redemption lies not in perishable things but in the precious blood of Christ. This is the hunger for God that grows as we contemplate the tension between the empty way of life handed down by our ancestors and the fullness of life offered to us by the one who was chosen before the creation of the world. Our yearning for true spiritual nourishment deepens as we set in contrast human frailty ("All people are like grass," 1 Pet 1:24) and human flourishing ("the word of the Lord endures forever," 1 Pet 1:25). The adult vices of malice, deceit, hypocrisy, envy, and slander are in tension with the innocence and purity of a baby's natural hunger for her mother's pure and unadulterated milk.

Peter based his ethical imperatives on the Old Testament. To set our hope on the grace to come is rooted in the prophets (1 Pet 1:10, 13). To be holy as God is holy comes from Leviticus (1 Pet 1:15–16; Lev 19:2). To be redeemed not with perishable things such as silver and gold but by the precious blood of Christ is drawn from Isaiah (Isa 52:3, 53). To live in reverent fear of the Lord because of the redemption of Christ, "a lamb without blemish or defect," recalls Numbers and Isaiah (1 Pet 1:19; Num 6:14; Isa 53:7). To love one another deeply is founded on Isaiah's description of the enduring word of the Lord (1 Pet 1:22; Isa 40:6–8), and Psalm 34:8 inspires the exhortation to crave real spiritual nourishment: "Taste and see that the Lord is good; blessed is the one who takes refuge in him." Peter is a New Testament apostle and an Old Testament theologian. His call to holiness takes in the full scope of salvation history and the pivotal meaning of Christ's redemptive sacrifice.

THE MIND MATTERS

Peter begins with a working-class metaphor: "Therefore, having girded up the loins of your mind set your hope on the grace to be brought to you when Jesus Christ is revealed in his coming" (1 Pet 1:13). If Peter were a coach challenging his players he might say, "Get your head in the game!" If he were a teacher or a manager he might say, "Roll up the sleeves of your mind." The mental image is of a Near Eastern laborer tucking up a long robe in his belt so that he could go about his work unhindered. Peter challenges believers to mentally and emotionally engage in the hard work of setting their hope on the grace of Christ.

Our translations are accurate ("with minds that are alert and fully sober," 1 Pet 1:13), but they miss Peter's graphic image intended for his hardworking recipients. The image is reminiscent of and may be drawn from the exodus, when the Israelites were prepared for an immediate departure following the Passover: "In this manner you shall eat it: your loins girded, your sandals on your feet, and your staff in your hand; you shall eat it in haste. It is the Lord's Passover" (Exod 12:11).

Hope in the gospel comes by "girding up the loins of your intelligence."[1] Calvin quipped that Peter "doubles the metaphor by ascribing loins to the mind."[2] Interestingly, the image is compatible with a modern adaptation. Neuroscientists tell us that we have a dual-processing brain, a synergistic interaction of reason and emotion, head and heart. Our hybrid brains trigger two kinds of responses, immediate emotional responses and reflective reasoned responses.[3] "Peter's double metaphor suggests that the mental activity required for hoping in Christ demands both preparation ("girding up") and exertion (working "the loins of the intelligence").[4]

Setting our hope on the grace of Christ involves a whole-brain response, engaging all four lobes of the cerebrum: (1) the frontal lobe is associated with reasoning, planning, parts of speech, movement, emotions, and problem solving; (2) the parietal lobe is associated with movement, orientation, recognition, and perception of stimuli; (3) the occipital lobe is associated with visual processing; and (4) the temporal lobe is associated with perception and recognition of auditory stimuli, memory, and speech. Every aspect of mental and emotional activity is gathered up and focused on the life and teaching of Christ. Peter's emphasis is entirely consistent with Paul's admonition, "Let this mind be in you which was also in Christ Jesus" (Phil 2:5), and "Do not conform to the pattern of this world, but be transformed by the renewing of your mind" (Rom 12:2).

The first recipients of Peter's letter differ from many in popular Christianity who presume that everything they need to know about the gospel can be learned in a simple "Jesus saves" sermon. They are fed a steady diet of sermonic clichés that only serve to starve the Christian mind of the Word. Preachers purposefully shy away from any intellectual challenge. They claim that anything beyond a "simple faith" is confusing and may prove harmful. The failure to apply the mind to biblical truth masquerades as sincere piety, but it is in fact a betrayal of the gospel.

---

1. Harink, *1 and 2 Peter*, 54.
2. Calvin, *Hebrews and 1 and 2 Peter*, 243.
3. Greene, *Moral Tribes*, 137.
4. Harink, *1 and 2 Peter*, 54.

Deep Obedience

Kayla grew up in northern Alabama and attended church all of her life. She said her minister back home preached three sermons no matter what Scripture passage he chose: God loves you and you need to accept Jesus; God loves you and you need to come to church; God loves you and if you don't love him back, you're going to hell. Guilt was the nagging motivator in her shallow subcultural Christianity. In her senior year of high school, her mother had an affair and her parents divorced. Kayla was in emotional pain from her parents' divorce, as well as getting over an abusive relationship, when she joined the Baptist fellowship at Vanderbilt University. For the first time she met thoughtful believers devoted to Jesus Christ. This opened up a whole new world for her. She discovered what it meant to follow the Lord Jesus. Kayla had to wait until college to discover the power and depth of the word of God. She suffered spiritual malpractice at the hands of a minister who abused the biblical text and distorted the Christian life.

One of my students described his early years in the faith this way:

> I am the product of the pop Evangelicalism of our current day. For most of my life I have sat in church while being inoculated with low levels of Christianity. With the IV-drip bag labeled "Self-Help Moralism" connected to one arm and "Daily Devotionalism" to the other arm, I spent much of my life drifting on the tenuous edge of a coma.... Like a waking dream, I was living the "Christian life." My world was one where the Bible had no power . . . and where preaching was like a giant pacifier. . . . We were deprived of true sustenance. In looking back, it is no wonder that I was depressed and contemplating suicide by the time I was twenty years old.[5]

These stories from the front lines of popular church culture indicate how far the church has strayed from good preaching and thoughtful spiritual direction. We need to let texts like 1 Peter back into the conversation. Pastors can serve as Silas did, and bring this spiritually and intellectually challenging exhortation into the life of the church. If we are going to rejoice greatly in our Trinity-shaped identity and Christ-protected security, we must know the truth of God's Word better than we do. Instead of mind-numbing religion we need a mind-engaging, Christ-centered obedience.

Peter follows up his challenge to engage the mind with a series of imperatives. We are exhorted to be holy, to fear the Lord, to love one another deeply, and to crave spiritual nourishment. Each imperative requires discernment and deep obedience. Each imperative is coupled with a rationale

---

5. Used with permission.

and motive. The foundation for this radical behavioral change is based squarely on the redemption found in the life-death-resurrection and glorification of Jesus Christ. He is the lamb that was chosen before the creation of the world. He is the imperishable seed—the living and enduring Word of God.

MIND OVER MOOD

First Peter's exhortation to set our hope on the grace that will be revealed in the coming of Jesus Christ reminds us of a point in Israel's history when personal autonomy and subjective opinion claimed the majority vote and the controlling interest. One line captures the spirit of the age then and now: "Everyone did as he saw fit" (Judg 17:6; 21:25). Or, as another version states, "Everyone did what was right in his own eyes" (KJV). Self-centered, authority-resistant individualism, with its spirit of self-indulgence and easy tolerance of evil, was a problem then as it is today.

Philosophers Hubert Dreyfus and Sean Kelly argue in *All Things Shining* that there are no deep and hidden truths to the universe, much less revealed truths. Humans may in fact be cosmic orphans, but that does not mean we have to live in despair. They turn to Homer's polytheism, or more precisely, Homer's "public and shareable moods" as a way forward through nihilistic despair.[6] Living is not about inner convictions and moral actions, as much as it is about being in sync with the gods and their moods.

According to Dreyfus and Kelly these moods attune us "to what matters most in a situation, allowing us to respond appropriately without thinking."[7] These two prominent philosophers claim that their ideal is the "unthinking heroic actor." The person who responds to the mood of the moment without thinking is the person best attuned to what truly matters in life. Wesley Autrey, the New York "Subway Hero," is their prime example. Without regard for his own life and without a moment's hesitation Wesley threw himself over the body of a young man who had fallen backward on the tracks as five train cars screeched over them. In the moment, according to Dreyfus and Kelly, Wesley Autrey embodied a true sense of the sacred. Like a wave whooshing up, such experiences offer a singular moment of exhilaration, leaving only a memory in their wake. In the whooshing up we catch a glimpse of focused meaning—a meaning that lies both outside of

---

6. Dreyfus and Kelly, *All Things Shining*, 60.
7. Ibid., 84.

us and within us. Dreyfus and Kelly see the potential for humans to create meaning out of nothing by allowing the situation itself to call forth action. Humans are best driven "not by some internal set of thoughts or desires, nor by a calculated set of plans or principles" but something outside of them, by the mood of the moment.[8] Thinking interferes with our freedom to respond as these moods dictate.

The influence of the moods is not limited to elite philosophers trying to rescue secular man from despair. Even Christians, who profess belief in universal truth and moral order, push back against the call to "be holy in all you do." It is popular in some Christian circles to encourage a "live and let live," "just be yourself," "don't let anyone tell you what to do" morality. The thought seems to be that Christians will spontaneously do the right thing. The Holy Spirit is credited with a "be yourself" ethic, as if the indwelling presence of the Spirit will automatically cause Christians to do what is right. The moral and ethical vision of the New Testament is ignored and the work of righteousness is equated with works righteousness. N. T. Wright observes,

> This whole way of thinking has become entrenched in many parts of our world, not least in many parts of many churches. Some people mistake it for the gospel itself, supposing that the romantic and existentialist rejection of rules is the same thing as Paul's doctrine of "justification by faith apart from works of the law," or the same thing as what Jesus was advocating when he confronted the law-bound Pharisees.[9]

Given human nature and our propensity to sin, holiness does not come naturally. To think and act Christianly about sex and intimacy, leisure and sports, success and money, will not happen if we are fed a steady diet of pop Christianity. The challenge to "take captive every thought to make it obedient to Christ" (2 Cor 10:5) involves a whole-brain response to the word of God and life.

Some time ago I led a seminar in moral medicine. The reaction of one of the medical doctors attending the seminar was fairly typical of how many Christians think about morality. He claimed that 99 percent of the time he goes about meeting the needs of his patients without ever facing a moral issue. He concluded that medical ethics was limited to controversial issues like abortion, euthanasia, genetic engineering, and surrogate motherhood.

---

8. Ibid., 6.
9. Wright, *After You Believe*, 51.

He resisted the idea that everything about medicine involves morality: our view of science and nature, the role of the servant-physician, the ethos of the medical profession, the purpose of technology, the accessibility of health care, the responsibilities of the patient, the care given to the dying, and the comfort offered to a grieving family. Nor did he realize that the Christian physician can make moral decisions on controversial issues like abortion and euthanasia, yet disobey God by treating diseases, not patients, serving himself above others, and trusting in his own self-sufficiency.

HOW WE SHOULD LIVE

When I served a church in San Diego we published two statements: *What We Believe* and *How We Should Live*. Many churches state their doctrinal positions, but far fewer describe their commitment to biblical obedience. We modeled our statement after Wheaton College's Community Covenant.[10] Our intention was to define our identity and our shared commitment as a biblical community. We wanted to clarify not only our beliefs but our practices. A few of the leaders challenged the notion of a community covenant. To them it seemed legalistic and works-oriented, but after prayer and discussion they came to see the need of affirming both our orthodoxy and our orthopraxy. What follows is that community covenant.

> The goal of our church is to live, work, serve, and worship together as a Household of Faith centered in the Lord Jesus Christ. Our mission is to make disciples, baptizing them in the name of the Father and of the Son and of the Holy Spirit, and teaching them to obey everything Christ has commanded.[11] We humbly and prayerfully accept the challenge to encourage the development of whole and effective Christians who will impact the church and society worldwide for Christ and His Kingdom. Along with the fellowship and blessings of participation in this Household of Faith come responsibilities. We seek to take seriously the whole counsel of God, because we are convinced that "all Scripture is God-breathed and is useful for teaching, rebuking, correcting and training in righteousness."[12]
> The biblical foundation of Christian community is expressed in Jesus' two great commandments: "Love the Lord your God with

---

10. Wheaton College Community Covenant, www.wheaton.edu/About-Wheaton/Community-Covenant. Used with permission.

11. Matt 28:19–20.

12. 2 Tim 3:16.

all your heart and with all your soul and with all your mind," and, "Love your neighbor as yourself." Jesus himself perfectly demonstrated the pattern: love for God, acted out in love for others. Acknowledging our dependence on the power and grace of God, the members of First Presbyterian Church of San Diego covenant to live according to this ideal.

The purposes of this community covenant are as follows:

–to cultivate a Body life in our church that encourages spiritual, moral, relational and intellectual growth.

–to integrate our lives around Christian principles and devotion to Jesus Christ.

–to remove whatever may hinder us from our calling as a Christ-centered biblical community.

–to encourage one another to see that living for Christ involves dependence on God's Spirit and obedience to the Bible, which is God's Word, rather than a passive acceptance of prevailing practices.

Affirming Biblical Standards

We desire to build this covenant on basic biblical standards for godly Christian character and behavior. We understand that our calling includes the following:

- The call to acknowledge the Lordship of Christ over all of life and thought, "so that in everything he might have the supremacy."[13] This involves a wholehearted obedience to Jesus and careful stewardship in all dimensions of life: our time, our possessions, our God-given capacities, our opportunities. We seek to "love the Lord our God with all our heart and with all our soul and with all our strength."[14] So that whatever we do, whether in word or deed, we do it all in the name of the Lord Jesus, giving thanks to God the Father through him.[15]

---

13. Col 1:18.
14. Deut 6:5.
15. Col 3:17.

- The call to love God with our whole being, including our minds, and to love our neighbor as ourselves.[16] Christlike love should be the motive in all decisions, actions, and relationships.[17]

- The call to pursue holiness in every aspect of our thought and behavior out of reverence for God.[18]

- The call to exercise our Christian freedom responsibly within the framework of God's Word, humbly submitting ourselves to one another with loving regard for the needs of others. Our desire should be to do nothing out of selfish ambition or vain conceit.[19]

- The call to treat our own bodies, and those of others, with the honor due the very temple of the Holy Spirit.[20]

- The call to participate in the life of church through worship, instruction, fellowship, prayer and serving others.[21]

LIVING THE CHRISTIAN LIFE

We believe these biblical standards will show themselves in a distinctly Christian way of life, an approach to living we expect of ourselves and of one another. This lifestyle involves practicing those attitudes and actions the Bible portrays as virtues and avoiding those the Bible portrays as sinful. Life in Christ was never meant to be reduced to a list of good works.

"For it is by grace [we] have been saved, through faith—and this not from [ourselves], it is the gift of God—not by works, so that no one can boast. For we are God's workmanship, created in Christ Jesus to do good works, which God prepared in advance for us to do."[22]

---

16. Matt 22:37-40.
17. Rom 13:8-10; 1 John 4:7-12.
18. 2 Cor 7:1; 1 Thess 4:7; Heb. 12:14; 1 Pet 1:15-16.
19. 1 Pet 5:5; Eph 5:21; Phil 2:3-11; Rom 14:1-23; 1 Thess 4:9.
20. 1 Cor 6:17-20.
21. Acts 2:42-47; Heb 10:25; 1 Thess 3:14-15.
22. Eph 2:8-10.

According to the Scriptures, followers of Jesus Christ will:

show evidence of the Holy Spirit who lives within them, such as "love, joy, peace, patience, kindness, goodness, faithfulness, gentleness and self-control;"[23]

"put on" compassion, kindness, humility, gentleness, patience, forgiveness, and supremely, love;[24]

seek righteousness, mercy and justice, particularly for the helpless and oppressed;[25]

love and side with what is good in God's eyes, and abhor what is evil in God's eyes;[26]

uphold the God-given worth of human beings, from conception to death, as the unique image-bearers of God;[27]

uphold chastity among the unmarried and the sanctity of marriage between a man and woman;[28]

be people of integrity whose word can be fully trusted;[29]

give faithful witness to the Gospel, practice good works toward all, and live lives of prayer and thanksgiving.[30]

---

23. Gal 5:22.
24. Col 3:12–14.
25. Prov 21:3; 31:8–9; Mic 6:8; Matt 23:23; Gal 6:10.
26. Amos 5:15; Rom 12:9; 16:19.
27. Gen 1:27; Ps 8:3–8.
28. 1 Cor 6:18; Heb 13:4.
29. Ps 15:4; Matt 5:33–37.
30. Acts 1:8; 1 Pet 3:15; Gal 6:10; Eph 2:10; Heb 10:24; 1 Pet 2:11; 1 Thess 5:17–18; Jas 5:16; Titus 2:8.

By contrast, Scripture condemns the following:

pride, dishonesty (such as stealing and lying), injustice, prejudice, immodesty in dress or behavior, slander, gossip, vulgar or obscene language, blasphemy, greed and materialism (which may manifest themselves in gambling, compulsive spending, self-indulgence), covetousness, the taking of innocent life, and illegal activities;[31]

hypocrisy, self-righteousness, and legalism, understood as the imposition of extra-biblical standards of godliness or the distortion of biblical standards of righteousness by one person or group upon another;[32]

sinful attitudes and behaviors such as "impurity and debauchery; idolatry and witchcraft; hatred, discord, jealousy, fits of rage, selfish ambition, dissensions, factions and envy; drunkenness, orgies, and the like;"[33]

sexual immorality, such as the use of pornography, pre-marital sex, adultery, homosexual behavior and all other sexual relations outside the bounds of marriage between a man and woman.[34]

Exercising Responsible Freedom

Beyond these explicit biblical issues, this Household of Faith seeks to foster the practice of responsible Christian freedom.[35] This requires a wise stewardship of mind, body, time, abilities and resources on the part of every member of the community. Responsible freedom also requires thoughtful, biblically-guided choices in matters of behavior, entertainment, interpersonal relationships, and observance of the Lord's Day. We seek to exercise our freedom responsibly, carefully, and in Christlike love. We seek to be a

---

31. Prov 16:18; 1 Cor 6:10; Exod 20:7; Rom 13:1–2,9; Col 3:8–9; Jas 2:13; Gal 3:26–29; 1 Tim 2:8–10; Heb 13:5–6.
32. Acts 15:5–11; Matt 16:6; 23:13–36.
33. Gal 5:19–21.
34. Matt 5:27–28; Rom 1:21–27; 1 Cor 6:9; Gen 2:24; Eph 5:31.
35. Gal 5:13–14; 1 Pet 2:16–17.

> healing community for those who suffer from emotional trauma, physical abuse, and substance abuse.
>
> This Household of Faith is committed to self-control, avoidance of harmful practices, the responsible use of freedom, sensitivity to the heritage and practices of other Christians, and honoring the name of Jesus Christ in all we do. We desire to be a covenant community of Christians marked by integrity, responsible freedom, and dynamic, Christlike love. Keeping our covenant may also on occasion require that we take steps to hold one another accountable, confronting one another in love as we work together to live in faithfulness both to God's biblical commands and to our own word. Such loving acts of confrontation are at times difficult, but when performed in the right spirit, they serve to build godly character for both the individuals involved and the community as a whole.[36] Only in this way, as we are willing to speak the truth in love, will we "grow up into him who is the Head, that is, Christ."[37]

Parents know that obedient children do not happen automatically. Heartfelt obedience requires careful parental nurture, a willing and receptive spirit in the child, and years of patience. No matter how old we are it is always challenging to be the Lord's obedient child. It is not our second nature to fear the Lord and love one another deeply. It is not in our DNA to be selfless and sacrificial. It takes hard work and years of prayerful discipline.

In Aldous Huxley's *Brave New World* people are conditioned to do what is expected of them. And if there is any trouble a pill is provided, called soma—designed "to give you a holiday from the facts." In Huxley's futuristic civilization there is always soma "to calm your anger, to reconcile you to your enemies, to make you patient and long-suffering." The "Controller" praises the benefits of soma:

> In the past you could only accomplish these things by making a great effort and after years of hard moral training. Now, you swallow two or three half-gramme tablets, and there you are. Anybody can be virtuous now. You can carry at least half your morality about in a bottle. Christianity without tears—that's what soma is.[38]

---

36. Gal 6:1; Matt 18:15–17.
37. Eph 4:15.
38. Huxley, *Brave New World*, 190.

David Livingstone, the nineteenth-century missionary, doctor, and explorer, describes a conversation he had with Chief Sekomi of the Bamangwato tribe:

> On one occasion Sekomi, having sat with me in the hut for some time in deep thought, at length addressing me by a pompous title said, "I wish you would change my heart. Give me medicine to change it, for it is proud, proud and angry, angry always." I lifted up the Testament and was about to tell him of the only way in which the heart can be changed, but he interrupted me by saying, "Nay, I wish to have it changed by medicine, to drink and have it changed at once, for it is very proud and very uneasy, and continually angry with someone." He then rose and went away.[39]

We may wish for a Christianity without tears, but it would certainly not be authentic Christianity. It might be religious, complete with Sunday services and doctrine, but it would fail to please Christ. There is no instant morality—no holiness pill. The deceptiveness of sin remains a threat from one end of the Christian life to the other.

A MIND-SET

In *After You Believe: Why Christian Character Matters*, N. T. Wright uses Captain "Sully" Sullenberger's emergency landing of US Airways flight 1549 on the Hudson River on January 15, 2009 to illustrate the effort involved in moral training. He draws an analogy between the hard work involved in mastering the skills necessary to land a plane in an emergency and the transformation of character necessary in following Jesus Christ.

Sullenberger was able to land that plane because of years of training, practice and professionally acquired skill. He and his copilot had three minutes to shut down the engines, set the right speed, and keep the nose of the plane just right. They had to disconnect the autopilot, override the flight management system, and activate the ditch system to seal the vents and make the plane as waterproof as possible. All the while "they had to fly and then glide the plane in a fast left-hand turn so that they could come down facing south, going with the flow of the river."[40] Then they had to level the wings and keep the nose just right so that they would land as flat

---

39. Seaver, *David Livingstone*, 58.
40. Wright, *After You Believe*, 19.

as possible. The reason Captain Sullenberger and his copilot performed so well that day was that they had trained for just such an emergency.

Peter knows that what he is asking believers to do is demanding. His one-line admonitions can be repeated easily, but only practiced with considerable effort.

"Do not conform to the evil desires you had when you lived in ignorance" (1 Pet 1:14).

"Be holy in all you do" (1 Pet 1:15).

"Live out your time as foreigners here in reverent fear" (1 Pet 1:17).

"Love one another deeply, from the heart" (1 Pet 1:22).

Nothing required here becomes "second nature" without tremendous spiritual, intellectual, and emotional effort. Of course, everything depends on being chosen by the triune God and being given new birth into a living hope. Everything depends on the sanctifying work of the Holy Spirit and the obedience of Jesus and his redemptive sacrifice. But with that said, Peter calls for total engagement. There is no divorce between salvation and sanctification. To be saved is to be sanctified. To be born again is to grow up in our salvation. This is why Peter likens old believers as well as young to newborns crying for their mother's milk. No matter how long we have followed Christ we need spiritual nourishment.[41]

There is more to this craving for nourishment than hearing sermons and attending Bible studies. Karen Jobes argues that Peter's "pure spiritual milk" metaphor underscores the real nature of the food necessary for genuine spiritual growth. The metaphors, such as the imperishable seed and pure spiritual milk, emphasize meaningful growth. It is not about exposure to Christian information or even adherence to the word of God, as much as it is about truly growing in the word of God. Christians are meant to crave the "divine grace on which all reborn believers must depend to sustain life in Christ."[42] The "milk" is the preached word of God (1 Pet 1:25) but more than that it is "the sustaining life of God given in mercy to his children."[43]

We ought to feel the tension between the adult vices that belong in our past and the new nonthreatening peaceable life we have in Christ. The personality and vocabulary of the old nature is characterized by malice,

---

41. Karen Jobes writes, "Although elsewhere in the NT milk is used as a metaphor for teachings suitable for immature Christians (Heb 5:12) or worldly Christians (1 Cor 3:1), such a negative connotation is not found here." Jobes, *1 Peter*, 132.

42. Jobes, *1 Peter*, 137.

43. Michaels, *1 Peter*, 89.

deceit, hypocrisy, envy, and slander, but the new nature in Christ is nourished on the "pure unadulterated" word of God. We want to get rid of even the hint of a wicked disposition that seeks the harm of others. We reject the hypocritical division between a public self and private self. We forbid the evil eye, filled as it is with envy and greed. We refuse to insult, "put down," "bad-mouth," or "disparage" others.[44] Peter's emphasis on *all* malice and *all* deceit and slander of *every kind* stresses a "no tolerance" policy for evil in the born-again Christian. When we "grow up in our salvation" it is evident in our speech and actions. There is no room here for a vindictive spirit or resentment. We see this emphasis on the word of God and ethical transformation throughout the New Testament (Rom 12:1–2; Jas 1:21; Col 3:12–17).

At the center of Peter's exhortation is the foundational and motivational truth of redemption based on the "precious blood of Christ, a lamb without blemish or defect" (1 Pet 1:19). Theology and ethics are integrated and the entire Christian community is challenged. Peter weaves together redemption's provision with redemption's purpose. We are never very far from the "reason for the hope [we] have" in Christ (1 Pet 3:15), which is always best revealed in a transformed life—a holy life.

---

44. Elliott, *1 Peter*, 398.

4

Living Stones

As you come to him, the living Stone—rejected by humans but chosen by God and precious to him—You also, like living stones, are being built into a spiritual household to be a holy priesthood, offering spiritual sacrifices acceptable to God through Jesus Christ. For in Scripture it says: "See, I lay a stone in Zion, a chosen and precious cornerstone, and the one who trusts in him will never be put to shame." Now to you who believe, this stone is precious. But to those who do not believe, "The stone the builders rejected has become the cornerstone," and, "A stone that causes people to stumble and a rock that makes them fall." They stumble because they disobey the message—which is also what they were destined for.

But you are a chosen people, a royal priesthood, a holy nation, God's special possession, that you may declare the praises of him who called you out of darkness into his wonderful light. Once you were not a people, but now you are the people of God; once you had not received mercy, but now you have received mercy. 1 Peter 2:4–10

Exhortation gives way to encouragement as Peter underscores the messianic community's no-shame identity, their no-fear solidarity, and their noncompetitive community. Peter quotes or alludes to seven Old Testament texts beginning with his allusion to Psalm 34 to describe the household of God:

> Those who look to him are radiant; their faces are never covered with shame.... Taste and see that the Lord is good; blessed is the one who takes refuge in him (Ps 34:5, 8).
>
> The stone the builders rejected has become the cornerstone; the Lord has done this and it is marvelous in our eyes (Ps 118:22–23).
>
> Now if you obey me fully and keep my covenant, then out of all nations you will be my treasured possession. Although the whole earth is mine, you will be for me a kingdom of priests and a holy nation (Exod 19:5–6).
>
> He will be a holy place; for both Israel and Judah he will be a stone that causes people to stumble and a rock that makes them fall (Isa 8:14).
>
> So this is what the Sovereign Lord says: "See, I lay a stone in Zion, a tested stone, a precious cornerstone for a sure foundation; the one who relies on it will never be stricken with panic" (Isa 28:16).
>
> The wild animals honor me, the jackals and owls, because I provide water in the wilderness and streams in the wasteland, to give drink to my people, my chosen, the people I formed myself that they might proclaim my praise (Isa 43:20–21).
>
> I will plant her for myself in the land; I will show my love to the one I called "Not my loved one." I will say to those called "Not my people," "You are my people"; and they will say, "You are my God" (Hos 2:23).

Drawing from the Psalms, the Prophets, and the Pentateuch, Peter underscores the theological significance of being rejected by humans but chosen by God. First Peter's recipients were the chosen outsiders who had been chosen by the foreknowledge of God, through the sanctifying work of the Holy Spirit, because of the obedience of Jesus Christ and the sprinkling of his blood. In the past they lived in moral and spiritual ignorance (darkness) and practiced an empty way of life (1 Pet 1:14, 18), but now in Christ they had tasted that the Lord is good.

These Old Testament texts recall the exodus, the exile, and the journey home to the promised land. In the past the home for the homeless was fulfilled in a return to their ancestral land, but in Jesus Christ the promised fulfillment has changed radically. The messianic community is no longer ethnically and geographically limited to Jews and Jerusalem. There is an open invitation to Jews and Gentiles, religious and secular alike, to come home to Jesus Christ. The return home is a continuous and exclusive coming to Jesus Christ. Home is anywhere where Jesus is, from Ulan Bator in Mongolia to a rural village in Ghana.

"As you come to him, the living Stone—rejected by humans but chosen by God and precious to him—you also, like living stones, are being built into a spiritual house . . ." (1 Pet 2:4–5). God takes what the world rejects and builds his household on the reality of Christ's resurrection. His promises belong to Jews and Gentiles, monotheists and idol worshipers alike. As the Lord said, "I will say to those called 'Not my people,' 'You are my people;' and they will say, 'You are my God.'"

THE LIVING STONE

Images of nursing babies and home construction do not clash but coalesce in Jesus Christ, the living stone.[1] Like his Lord, Peter mines in a single metaphor a rich deposit of theological gold drawn from the Old Testament, the teaching of Jesus, the memory of his personal encounter with Jesus, his defense before the Sanhedrin, and the theology of the apostles.

The imagery of the rock has deep roots in the Old Testament. Moses declared, "Oh, praise the greatness of our God! He is the Rock, his works are perfect, and all his ways are just" (Deut 32:3–4). In David's last words, he praised the God of Israel, saying, "the Rock of Israel said to me: 'When one rules over people in righteousness, when he rules in the fear of God, he is like the light of morning at sunrise on a cloudless morning, like the brightness after rain that brings grass from the earth'"(2 Sam 23:3–4; see also Isa 30:29). The psalmist exclaims, "O Lord, my Rock and my Redeemer" and "Truly he is my rock and my salvation" (Ps 19:14; 62:2, 6–7). For Peter the metaphor of the rock captures the fullness of the triune God.

Jesus used parables to reveal his messianic self-understanding. He applied Old Testament images for God to himself. He designated himself as the sower, the director of the harvest, the rock, the shepherd, the bridegroom, the father, the giver of forgiveness, the vineyard owner, the lord, and the king. Each of these images represents a significant association with God and his work found in the Old Testament. Jesus used the image of the rock to conclude the Sermon on the Mount. To respond to him and his words was to respond to God himself. The metaphor of the rock was critical

---

1. In the messianic Psalms (23:4–5 and 19:4–5) we see a similar juxtaposition of images.

for Peter's own self-identity. Moments after he confessed "You are the Messiah, the Son of the living God," Jesus said:

> "Blessed are you, Simon son of Jonah, for this was not revealed to you by flesh and blood, but by my Father in heaven. And I tell you that you are Peter, and on this rock I will build my church, and the gates of Hades will not overcome it. I will give you the keys of the kingdom of heaven; whatever you bind on earth will be bound in heaven, and whatever you loose on earth will be loosed in heaven" (Matt 16:16–19).

There is a striking convergence of identities: Jesus is the rock and Peter is the rock. In Christ, Peter is the rock upon whom the church is built. First Peter underscores that relationship. "As you come to him, the living Stone . . . you also, like living stones are being built into a spiritual house . . ." (1 Pet 2:4–5). Jesus embodied the kingdom and fulfilled its agenda (Luke 4:18–19). He personified the rule of God. He did what only God could do: he forgave sins, performed miracles, and claimed absolute authority in his teaching. But surprisingly, everything he claimed for himself he gave to his disciples. He gave to Peter, the representative disciple, "the keys of the kingdom of heaven," with the redemptive and judgmental significance of the gospel (Matt 16:19; Luke 22:29). He sent his disciples out to fish for people (Mark 1:17). He gave them authority to preach, cast out demons (Mark 3:14–15), and "make disciples of all nations" (Matt 28:19). The one who received the Spirit without limit promised that "anyone who has faith in me will do what I have been doing. He will do even greater things than these, because I am going to the Father" (John 14:12; see Joel 2:28–29). More important than power, however, is the familial intimacy with the Father (Luke 10:20). He who called God "Abba" gives us the "the Spirit of sonship," by whom we cry, "Abba, Father" (Rom 8:15).

Jesus used the imagery of the rock to explain his rejection. "Haven't you read this passage of Scripture?" he asked the religious authorities. "The stone the builders rejected has become the cornerstone; the Lord has done this, and it is marvelous in our eyes" (Mark 12:10–11; see Ps 118:22–23). This is what Peter used in his defense before the Sanhedrin following Pentecost:

> It is by the name of Jesus Christ of Nazareth, whom you crucified but whom God raised from the dead, that this man stands before you healed. Jesus is "the stone you builders rejected, which has become the cornerstone." Salvation is found in no one else, for

there is no other name under heaven given to mankind by which we must be saved (Acts 4:10–12).

The Apostle Paul referenced the "rejected stone" in Romans to explain the failure of those who pursue works of righteousness: "They stumble over the stumbling stone, as it is written: See, I lay in Zion a stone that causes people to stumble and a rock that makes them fall, and the one who believes in him will never be put to shame" (Rom 9:32–33; see Isa 8:14; 28:16). In Ephesians he compared Jesus Christ to "the chief cornerstone" upon whom "the whole building is joined together" (Eph 2:20–22).

THE STONE THE BUILDERS REJECTED

Peter used the image of the rock to emphasize three truths: Jesus' oneness with God the Father; his oneness with his disciples; and his unwarranted but prophesied rejection. He drew a parallel between the living Stone and the living stones. "The experience and destiny of those who come to Christ are bound up with the experience and destiny of Christ himself."[2] Since Jesus was "the stone the builders rejected," his followers will suffer rejection along with him. In the eyes of the world we are outsiders, resident aliens, and foreigners. We are strangers in our home culture, but we have a spiritual house built by Christ.

Peter does not elaborate on the specific nature or cost suffered by these early Christians for following Christ. He gives no stories of painful family separation or job loss because of a person's faith and trust in Christ. There are no reports of anyone being thrown out of the Jewish synagogue or beaten up because they refused to pay homage to the gods of the guild. Incidents such as these may have been routine, but Peter chose not to report them. By identifying Christ's disciples as "exiles," "foreigners," and "strangers," Peter acknowledged the social turmoil experienced by Christ's followers. Both Jews and Gentiles who came to Christ were facing social opposition, ostracism, and estrangement. But state-sponsored violent persecution and martyrdom does not appear to describe the situation.

Peter does not minimize their suffering, but he insists on pointing to its value to test and reveal faithfulness. He likens "grief in all kinds of trials" to a refiner's fire that proves the genuineness of their faith (1 Pet 1:6–7). He admonishes and prepares believers for suffering but he does this without

---

2. Jobes, *1 Peter*, 148.

blaming the world and inciting hostility. "Dear friends," he warns, "do not be surprised at the fiery ordeal that has come on you to test you, as though something strange were happening to you. But rejoice inasmuch as you participate in the sufferings of Christ . . ." (1 Pet 4:12–13).

By refusing to tell persecution stories Peter shows a reluctance to foster a victim mentality among his recipients. His restraint checks a tempting way of endearing himself to his readers by identifying and elaborating on their suffering. Peter wants the emphasis elsewhere, not on how bad the culture is or on how badly Christians have been treated, but on how wonderful it is to be belong to the household of God. He frames his description of suffering not as an accusation against the culture, but as a potential opportunity for witness. The potential problems are hypothetical: "though they accuse you of doing wrong, they may see your good deeds . . ." (1 Pet 2:12); "But even if you should suffer for what is right, you are blessed" (1 Pet 3:14); and "If you are insulted because of the name of Christ, you are blessed for the Spirit of glory and of God rests on you" (1 Pet 4:14).

THE HOUSE OF THE SPIRIT

Christ's followers (living stones) are being built by God into a spiritual household, literally a house of the Spirit, to be a holy priesthood offering sacrifices "controlled and animated by God's sanctifying Spirit."[3] These sacrifices are initiated and guided by the Holy Spirit and are acceptable to God through the mediation of Jesus Christ.[4] Peter's household of faith language underscores the relational nature of the body of Christ.[5] As in the opening salutation there is an emphasis on the elect exiles being chosen by the triune God.

---

3. Elliott, *1 Peter*, 418.

4. Ibid., 113–15. Elliott writes, "There is in 1 Peter a more extensive and consistent employment of oikos-related terminology and imagery than in any other writing in the NT." *1 Peter*, 115. Elliott identifies seven words in the *Oikos* word group: παροικίας—1:17; οἶκος—2:5, 4:17; οἰκοδομεῖσθε—2:5; παροίκους—2:11; οἰκέται—2:18; συνοικοῦντες—3:7; οἰκονόμοι—4:10.

5. Snodgrass, *Ephesians*, 136. This emphasis on the household of God can also be seen in Ephesians 2:19–22. With the literary care of a poet, the Apostle Paul orchestrated a wordplay on the Greek word for "house" (οικος). In Christ we are no longer *aliens* (πάροικοι), but members of God's *household* (οἰκεῖοι), *built on* (ἐποικοδομηθέντες) a sure foundation, and the *building* (οἰκοδομὴ) is *built together* (συνοικοδομεῖσθε) into a *dwelling place* (κατοικητήριον) of God.

Believers in northern Ghana may have a deeper appreciation for what it meant for first-century Jews and Gentiles in Asia Minor to follow Christ than many Western believers. To be redeemed by Christ from "the empty way of life handed down to you from your ancestors" was bound to produce social alienation and hostility (1 Pet 1:18). In a tribal culture the community comes first and the individual comes second. The pressure to conform and comply with cultural customs, rituals, and taboos is great. To align oneself with a Christian world view that is antithetical to the prevailing cultural ethos is costly. Christians suffer social alienation, ridicule, slander, accusations, and shame. This is why Peter stressed the believer's new community—the household of God. This is why he quoted from the prophet Isaiah, "See, I lay a stone in Zion, a chosen and precious cornerstone, and the one who trusts in him will never be put to shame" (Isa 28:16).

Peter's description of our "new tribe" identity is powerful. God builds us into a community inspired and guided by the Holy Spirit, to become "a holy priesthood, offering spiritual sacrifices acceptable to God through Jesus Christ" (1 Pet 2:5). The "new tribe" community is rooted in the ancient tradition of Israel, established in Christ, and commissioned for global impact.

Believers in northern Ghana, like the recipients of Peter's letter, embrace this noncompetitive community more easily than Westerners. The triune God offers a no-shame identity and a no-fear solidarity in the household of God. But Western believers struggle with this God-given reality. We are steeped in individualism and personal autonomy. We are little chiefs with multiple tribal identities: family, school, work, sports, hobbies, church, friends, and entertainment. We are overcommitted, overworked, and overbusy. Competitive individualism leaves us empty and easily overwhelmed. Church is one small compartment in this competitive environment. Our multiple tribal identities, each with its own set of cultural customs, rituals, offerings, and obligations, compete for our loyalty. Colleagues at work, next door neighbors, workout friends, and even family members may not even know we belong to the new tribe. In a village in northern Ghana, steeped in ancient animism and rituals, a believer's commitment to Jesus Christ cannot be kept secret. Christ's followers become "outsiders" overnight.

Pollster George Barna prides himself on mapping the latest trends on the religious landscape. He predicts "an unprecedented reengineering of America's faith" due to widespread disillusionment with the megachurch. A new generation of believers "refuse to follow people in ministry leadership positions who cast a personal vision rather than God's, who seek popularity rather than the proclamation of truth in their public statements, or who are more concerned about their own legacy than that of Jesus Christ. They refuse to donate one more dollar to man-made monuments that mark their own achievements and guarantee their place in history."[6] Barna encourages believers to leave the local church and form their own models of spiritual intimacy, accountability, and service. In the future he sees believers "choosing from a proliferation of options, weaving together a set of favored alternatives into a unique tapestry that constitutes the personal 'church' of the individual."[7]

Barna shrinks the vision of the church down to the autonomous individual believer, who embraces what he or she wants to do. If playing golf on Sunday lowers your stress and helps you reflect more thoughtfully on the Bible, then skipping corporate worship is God's will for you. Barna's reasoning is simple enough: Who needs the hassles of the local church, anyway? The autonomous individual self can be a denomination of one. Instead of challenging competitive individualism, Barna offers believers a competitive strategy.

Peter envisioned a different kind of community, a household of faith built by God out of living stones—lives transformed by the grace of Christ. He never could have imagined popular Christianity's institutional church and its entertaining worship. The account below describes what many Christians are experiencing.

> I attended a "hip" church in the Bay Area. I didn't miss a Sunday. It was great entertainment. It was fun. And it was easy. There was no suggestion that being a Christian would require any effort on my part. Show up on Sunday, watch the show, and off you go. I'm sure that if I had tried, I could have found the message of the Cross, the true requirements needed to follow Jesus' message, and the reality of the Christian life.... But it wasn't obvious. It was a drop-in-and-be-entertained-for-an-hour-so-you-can-say-you-are-Born-Again church.
>
> I attended that church at a critical point in my life; at a time when I would be asked to make many serious decisions about life. I bear full responsibility for choosing that church, but it was the worst possible place for me. I got the message that all of life was to be easy and entertaining, including the center of my life, my faith.

6. Barna, *Revolution*, 14.
7. Ibid., 66.

As you might guess, almost every decision I made was based on a fast-food, convenience-store, quick fix, get-rich, and above all, feel-good-all-the-time mentality. Fifteen years ago I found myself in a non-marriage, making lots of money, addicted to alcohol, and miserable because of all those quick-fix decisions.

It's wonderful that no matter what mistakes we make Jesus forgives us and is waiting for us! No matter how many wrong turns we take, God is waiting for us. I realize now how far I had drifted from the ten-year-old boy who accepted Jesus as his savior. I don't like the [term] "Born Again" because it reminds me of the fast-fix lifestyle that got me where I was. I returned to God and I began to make decisions based on what Jesus would have me do. The changes have been remarkable. The un-wife is gone, the money is gone, the alcohol is gone, and above all the misery is gone. It has been replaced by joy. Joy was something that was gone from my life; it is back.[8]

My friend had to be converted from popular Christianity to Christ! He had to come out of the church to find Christ. Peter envisioned a spiritual house built on Jesus Christ, the "chosen and precious cornerstone." Not a ceremonial cornerstone, inscribed with the date of the building, or the capstone crowning the top of the building, but "the primary load-bearing stone that determined the lines of the building."[9] In the competition of tribal identities, cultural loyalties, and personal commitments, Christ wins absolutely. The stone is either precious or it is rejected. There are no divided loyalties; no clever balancing acts; no part-time Christians. If sports is your cornerstone, admit it. If work is your cornerstone, face it. If sex or money or politics or popularity is your cornerstone, own it. But we know this: "The stone the builders rejected has become the cornerstone" (Ps 118:22).

Rejection involves both disbelief and disobedience. Peter writes, "They stumble because they disobey the message—which is also what they were destined for" (1 Pet 2:8). To believe is to obey and to obey is to believe. It is not enough to say to Jesus, "Lord, Lord" and then refuse to do the will of the Father (Matt 7:21). "One cannot simply step over Jesus to go on about the daily routine and pass him by to build a future."[10] There is no room in Peter's description for nominal Christianity. You are either a living stone or you stumble and fall.

8. Used with permission.
9. Snodgrass, *Ephesians*, 137.
10. Goppelt, *A Commentary on 1 Peter*, 146.

THE PEOPLE OF GOD

If Peter had been a musician he would have used the full orchestra to bring his message to a crescendo.[11] "One of the striking features of this letter" is that Peter employed "the plethora of collective terms and images" to emphasize "the community-forming dynamic of salvation and the communal identity of the redeemed."[12] But one particular word is missing. "First Peter is one of the most church-oriented writings in the New Testament, though the word "church" (ἐκκλησία) never occurs."[13] Peter intentionally avoided the Greek word ἐκκλησία and its connotation of a public assembly (Acts 19:32, 39, 41). He distinguished the household of faith as God's called-out holy community. This "chosen race, royal priesthood, holy nation, and God's special possession" (1 Pet 2:5) was not to be confused with pagan assemblies.

If Peter were alive today he might wish to avoid using the word *church* altogether. The term has all but lost its meaningful association with the followers of Christ and in the mind of many refers to institutional religion. *Church* has become a worldly term and does not come close nine times out of ten in describing the holy community envisioned by Peter. The apostle identifies the believing community in such a way as to make an audience of admirers impossible.

In the tradition of exodus Israelites and Babylonian exiles, Peter affirmed that the followers of Christ had become a new race. They were a set-apart holy people redeemed by "the precious blood of Christ, a lamb without blemish or defect" (1 Pet 1:19). Church was not a mixed gathering of Christians and non-Christians who assembled weekly to hear an introduction to the gospel. Church was the priestly community meeting for worship and fellowship. Non-Christians were graciously welcomed but when they walked through the door they entered into a radically different culture, one that was not designed to cater to their felt needs, much less entertain them. They experienced a noncompetitive counterculture whose members shared a no-shame identity and a no-fear solidarity. They were befriended in a missional community dedicated to engaging the world for Christ and his kingdom.

---

11. Eugene Boring writes, "This passage presents one of the most dense constellations of ecclesiological imagery in the New Testament." Boring, *1 Peter*, 98.

12. Elliott, *1 Peter*, 113.

13. Ibid., 112.

Peter drew on the rich imagery of the Old Testament to describe the people of God. Four phrases encompass Peter's comprehensive description of the people of God. These four descriptive phrases ought to have an impact in the twenty-first century. They encompass the four dimensions of the new society in Christ: race, spirituality, politics, and community.

(1) A Chosen People

The phrase "my people" has an ethnic ring to it, but Peter used it to refer to the people of God drawn from every nation, tribe, people, and language (Rev 7:9). Peter recalled God's promise of deliverance to the Babylonian exiles and he applied the promise to the "elect exiles" (1 Pet 1:1). God promised to provide streams in the desert, to "give drink to my people, my chosen, the people I formed for myself that they may proclaim my praise" (Isa 43:20–21). Christ's redemption destroys ethnic privilege and pride of race. No person, group, race, tribe, or nation has the right to feel morally superior to others. The identity, calling, solidarity, and significance of the people of God is not based on ethnicity, family, heritage, or merit, but on Christ's atoning once-and-for-all sacrifice. The one new humanity formed in Christ is not part Jewish and part Gentile, nor is it part black and part white. This new race is an act of creation, not a mixture of Asian and Arab, Latin and European. God's "chosen people" were not meant to divide along ethnic, cultural, racial, social, gender, and generational lines. Since the Christian community is founded solely on Jesus Christ, it is a spiritual reality. This solidarity transcends sociological and psychological compatibility. It is the house of the Spirit, built by the Father on the cornerstone of the Son.

(2) A Royal Priesthood

God's promises to the Exodus Israelites are fulfilled in the lives of the "chosen outsiders" and "resident aliens." The word of the Lord through the patriarch Moses, "You will be for me a kingdom of priests" (Exod 19:6), is now God's word through the Apostle Peter: "You are a royal priesthood" (1 Pet 2:5). If believers are collectively identified as priests to the king of the universe, how can they feel like victims? The followers of Christ are holy and set apart for priestly service to the King of kings and Lord of lords. There is no higher calling than this; no special designation that ranks anyone higher than this God-ordained responsibility. The biblical concept of the priesthood of all believers stresses the equality and body-life of the church as a whole. When the emphasis does not fall on the "all" in the company of the "whole," but on the individual (the priesthood of the believer), the distortion can become an excuse for legitimizing individualistic opinion and justifying willful power plays in the congregation.

The book of Hebrews roots our priesthood in the priestly sacrifice of Jesus Christ, our great high priest, who was "tempted in every way, just as we are—yet he did not sin." He "learned obedience by the things that he suffered." (Heb 4:15; 5:8). Instead of the blood of sacrificial animals, he offered himself as a once-and-for-all perfect sacrifice. His blood "cleanses our consciences from acts that lead to death, so that we may serve the living God!" Christ is the mediator of a new covenant, rendering the old covenant obsolete, putting an end to the old sacrificial system, and giving us all the confidence "to enter the Most Holy Place by the blood of Jesus" (Heb 8:13; 10:1–4, 19).

The "royal priesthood" follows naturally from the new covenant. The author of Hebrews repeats Jeremiah's new covenant prophecy:

> I will put my laws in their minds and write them on their hearts. I will be their God, and they will be my people. No longer will they teach their neighbors, or say to one another, "Know the Lord," because they will all know me, from the least of them to the greatest. For I will forgive their wickedness and will remember their sins no more (Heb 8:10–12).

Consequently, the old order is gone. The priest's performance of religious duties is no longer necessary and the whole old sacrificial system is fulfilled in Jesus' once-and-for-all perfect sacrifice on our behalf. Instead of a special class of priests, we have a congregation of priests. "For there is one God and one mediator between God and human beings, Christ Jesus, himself human, who gave himself as a ransom for all people" (1 Tim 2:5–6). The new priesthood belongs to all who have been united through faith in Jesus Christ and all share in offering up sacrifices. But these sacrifices are no longer animals or grains, but ourselves and our praise (Rom 12:1; Heb 13:15–16). All believers are encouraged to "offer to God a sacrifice of praise—the fruit of lips that openly profess his name"(Heb 13:15).

(3) A Holy Nation

The recipients of 1 Peter lived under imperial and local political authorities. Fidelity to Christ and the holiness he commanded invariably led to cultural conflict and social estrangement, not because Christians were revolutionaries or separatists, but because their holiness was perceived as a social and political threat. Their life together as the people of God produced social alienation. The phrase "holy nation" or "holy people" is drawn from the Lord's instructions to Moses:

> Now if you obey me fully and keep my covenant, then out of all the nations you will be my treasured possession. Although the whole earth is mine, you will be for me a kingdom of priests and a holy nation (Exod 19:5–6).

Christ's followers knew that their hope was not in Rome or in the local tribal deities or in the gods of their local professional guilds. They were born again into a living hope. The people of God living in America would be better off if they understood that they could not put their hope in American politics or in the American economy. Some Christians talk as if they have no other identity or loyalty other than America, and when things don't go their way politically they are filled with anger and fear. Tim Keller writes, "This may be a reason why so many people now respond to U.S. political trends in such an extreme way.... They become agitated and fearful for the future. They have put the kind of hope in their political leaders and policies that once was reserved for God and the work of the gospel."[14]

The vitriolic rhetoric and slander expressed by Christians against politicians is an indication not of strength and boldness, but of fear and hate. Frustrated Christians feel that their culture is slipping away from them in spite of their best efforts to "bring back America" and "change the world for Christ." For many, the American Dream stands for the pursuit of happiness, individual rights, and democratic rule. The national ideology is materialistic and pluralistic, dedicated to a form of tolerance that is intolerant of absolute truth claims.

The Christian before the world is like Jesus before Pilate. Believers need to hear these words over and over again to stay on mission: "My kingdom is not of this world. If it were, my servants would fight to prevent my arrest by the Jewish leaders. But now my kingdom is from another place" (John 18:36).

---

14. Keller, *Counterfeit Gods*, 99.

What was true for the believers in Asia Minor is true for believers in America. If we have any hope of redeeming our witness, we will have "to disentangle the life and identity of the church from the life and identity of American society." James Hunter continues,

> For conservatives and progressives alike, Christianity far too comfortably legitimates the dominant political ideologies and far too uncritically justifies the prevailing macroeconomic structures and practices of our time.... The moral life and everyday social practices of the church are also far too entwined with the prevailing normative assumptions of American culture.... Christianity has uncritically assimilated to the dominant ways of life in a manner dubious at the least. Even more, these assimilations arguably compromise the fundamental integrity of its witness to the world.[15]

We cannot identify any nation or ideology with God's "holy nation" or Christ's kingdom on earth. The argument for American exceptionalism is not grounded in the word of God, but in a political ideology and agenda that misunderstands the impact of the gospel. The gospel is a countercultural movement that will remain a voice crying in the wilderness of an evil and broken culture. The people of God should not expect to be a controlling voice of culture, but they should aim to impress the world with Christ's goodness.

(4) A Special Possession

From the world's perspective Christ's followers are "outsiders," but from God's perspective they are "insiders." They are God's "treasured possession" (Exod 19:5) and his "chosen people" (Isa 43:21). Peter links the exodus Israelites to the Babylonian exiles to the elect exiles as one continuous covenant community called to "declare the praises of him who called you out of darkness into his wonderful light" (1 Pet 2:9). These "chosen outsiders" and "resident aliens" form a noncompetitive holy community. They have not been called of God to flee the world or fight the world. They have not been called to withdraw into their own tight-knit culture. They are not separatists, narrow-minded and opinionated. They do not impress the world as hostile and rigid and angry. Their form of offense, the offense of the cross, is the most winsome and attractive "offensiveness" that human culture has ever known.

15. Hunter, *To Change the World*, 184–85.

Peter's declarative and definitive definition of the people of God as a chosen people, a royal priesthood, a holy nation, and God's special possession recalls Jesus' words in the Sermon on the Mount, when he said, "You are the salt of the earth. . . . You are the light of the world" (Matt 5:13–14). Beatitude-based believers are God's "elect exiles." They belong to God's kingdom, experience God's comfort, and will inherit God's earth. They have been blessed with God's righteousness and they are defined by God's mercy, vision, identity, and reward. What more could God give them? They have it all, and for that reason they *are* salt and light. "'You folks *are*,' not 'You folks *ought* to be,' the most significant people on the planet."[16]

To conclude this section Peter draws on the Prophet Hosea and Yahweh's love story. Only now the prophecy first intended for Israel is transposed to include the Gentiles as well as the Jews. Hosea envisioned a new day and new relationship, a marriage conceived in everlasting love and founded on righteousness and justice, love and compassion. "'In that day,' declares the Lord, 'you will call me "my husband"; you will no longer call me "my master" ["my Baal"]. I will remove the names of the Baals from their lips; no longer will their names be invoked" (Hos 2:16–17). Yahweh's love poetry to Israel is now applied to the people of God drawn from every tribe, nation, people, and language.

> I will betroth you to me forever;
> I will betroth you in righteousness and justice,
> in love and compassion.
> I will betroth you in faithfulness,
> and you will acknowledge the Lord (Hos 2:19–20).

The apostles developed this prophecy of hope and applied its fulfillment to the followers of Christ. The day was coming when the terrible estrangement between Israel and Yahweh, which was publicized in the names of Hosea's children, would be overturned. "I will say to those called 'Not my people,' 'You are my people'; and they will say, 'You are my God'" (Hos 2:23). Like Peter, the Apostle Paul quoted these words to believers in Rome to affirm the gospel's outreach to the Gentiles. What was true for Israel was now true for Gentiles (Rom 9:25–26). Peter declares the fulfillment of Hosea's ancient prophecy to the "elect exiles," these "chosen outsiders" who are scattered throughout the hinterland of Asia Minor. "Once you were not

---

16. Bruner, *Matthew*, 1:188.

a people, but now you are the people of God; once you had not received mercy, but now you have received mercy" (1 Pet 2:10).

5

Resident Aliens

Dear friends, I urge you, as foreigners and exiles, to abstain from sinful desires, which wage war against your soul. Live such good lives among the pagans that, though they accuse you of doing wrong, they may see your good deeds and glorify God on the day he visits us.

Submit yourselves for the Lord's sake to every human authority: Whether to the emperor, as the supreme authority, or to governors, who are sent by him to punish those who do wrong and to commend those who do right. For it is God's will that by doing good you should silence the ignorant talk of foolish people.

Live as free people, but do not use your freedom as cover-up for evil; live as God's slaves. Show proper respect to everyone, love the family of believers, fear God, honor the emperor. 1 Peter 2:11–17

First Peter's synergy between theological identity and ethical challenge rests exclusively on the work and example of Christ. The interplay between encouragement and exhortation sets up a pivotal tension between social impact and Christian solidarity. Although Peter referred to his letter as brief, Silas may have spent days "debriefing" and instructing its original recipients.

Silas made his extensive 2,000-mile journey as a missionary-theologian. He traveled from Rome to Amisus on the Black Sea and then all the way south to Sardis before heading north to Nicomedia. At each gathering of Christians along the way, we envision Silas expounding the message of 1 Peter. As we enter into a similar analysis and application we follow in his steps.

Having laid down a solid foundation on hope (1 Pet 1:3–13), holiness (1 Pet 1:13–2:3), and the household of God (1 Pet 2:4–10), Peter turns to the critical and practical issue of how Christ's followers are to relate to culture (1 Pet 2:11–4:11). At the heart of his letter he delivers the heart of his message (1 Pet 2:11–12), followed by its costly relational application in various spheres of culture: political (1 Pet 2:13–17), economic (1 Pet 2:18–20), and familial (1 Pet 3:1–7). Peter relies solely on Christ and his example for the rationale and motivation for supporting his approach to culture. "To this you were called, because Christ suffered for you, leaving you an example, that you should follow in his steps" (1 Pet 2:21).

PASTORAL CARE

Peter's description of the people of God (1 Pet 2:9–10) rules out a pecking order of spiritual authority. He does not approach the "resident aliens" of Asia Minor as an ecclesiastical power figure who should be listened to because he holds an important office. Sadly, tradition has not embraced Peter's New Testament model. The church, like any other human institution, moved quickly toward worldly power and control. Denominational politics and the religious bureaucracy are the weak and inferior substitutes for pastoral humility and biblical spiritual direction.

"Dear friends" says all that needs to be said about Peter's authority. He addresses these believers as "beloved" even though it is likely that he has not met them. Nevertheless they share an intimate bond in Christ. They are "foreigners" and "exiles" scattered throughout Asia Minor. They are farmers, herdsmen, homemakers, weavers, and miners. For the first time in this letter Peter uses the first person singular: "I exhort [urge] you" (1 Pet 2:11). The word *exhort* conveys more than "request" but less than "command."[1] It is a word that combines recommendation and encouragement.[2]

He urges them "to abstain from sinful desires, which wage war against your soul" (1 Pet 2:11). Like a physician treating a life-or-death condition, Peter challenges believers to avoid the deadly cravings that threaten to devastate life. He uses a military term to underscore the deadly nature of this spiritual warfare. Then, he balances the negative admonition with the positive: "Live such good lives among the pagans[3] that, though they accuse

---

1. Elliott, *1 Peter*, 457.
2. Rom 12:1; Eph 4:1; 1 Thess 4:1, 10; 5:14; 2 Thess 3:12; 1 Tim 6:2; Titus 2:6, 15.
3. ἔθνεσιν is a collective term for all non-believers, including Jews and Gentiles.

you of doing wrong, they may see your good deeds and glorify God on the day he visits us" (1 Pet 2:12). The rest of the letter will focus on these "good deeds" and how this Christ-honoring, slander-silencing goodness is to be worked out in the political, social, and familial spheres of life. Peter keeps the eschatological vision of fulfillment and glory in the forefront of their minds (1 Pet 1:5, 7; 4:7, 17; 5:1, 10). But what is clear is that this biblical eschatology inspires rather than mitigates the ethical and sociological impact of the gospel.

Like his Lord, Peter is focused on cultural engagement, not withdrawal. His letter is excellent commentary on the Sermon on the Mount. Peter's spiritual direction resonates with Beatitude-based believers who have salt and light impact. These are believers who have chosen love instead of hate, purity instead of lust, fidelity instead of infidelity, honesty instead of dishonesty, reconciliation instead of retaliation, and prayer instead of revenge (Matt 5:1–48). Peter's earlier emphasis on deep obedience, "so be holy in all you do; for it is written: 'Be holy, because I am holy'" (1 Pet 1:15; Lev 19:2), is in sync with the Master's "Be perfect, therefore, as your heavenly Father is perfect" (Matt 5:48). The way of righteousness is not a vague, ethereal, other-worldly ethic. Jesus and his disciples define righteousness in a specific and definite way. We are not left to our whims and preferences but to the Spirit's revelation.

Jesus designed the power of evangelism to be rooted in his kingdom ethic embodied in the household of God. This is why the harmony between Jesus' teaching and the rest of the New Testament is so important. Peter and the other apostles are on the same page. The deeper we study the New Testament the more we see the Spirit's harmony. Peter could say "Amen" to Paul's admonition:

> I urge you, brothers and sisters, in view of God's mercy, to offer your bodies as living sacrifices, holy and pleasing to God—this is your true and proper worship. Do not conform to the pattern of this world, but be transformed by the renewing of your mind. Then you will be able to test and approve what God's will is—his good, pleasing and perfect will (Rom 12:1–2).

To offer our bodies as living sacrifices, holy and pleasing to God, is to take every aspect of our life and being and offer it to God. The whole self is to be given over to Christ: intellectually, emotionally, physically and spiritually. When the twelfth-century monk Bernard became abbot of Clairvaux in his mid-twenties, he told novices that they must leave their bodies outside the gates of the monastery.[4] The deeper spiritual life, he insisted, had to do with the soul, not with the body. The New Testament sees it differently. To "live such good lives among the pagans . . . that they see your good deeds" (1 Pet 2:12) requires a holistic response. We are to love the Lord our God with our whole being and our neighbor as ourselves. Christians believe there is a physical side to being spiritual and a spiritual side to being physical. The correlation belongs to the fact that we are made body, mind, and soul in God's image. We are neither bodyless souls nor soulless bodies, but bodies and souls in community.

Peter addresses "foreigners" and "strangers." He expects believers to see themselves as resident aliens and "chosen outsiders" even in their home culture. *The Message* begins this section, "Friends, this world is not your home, so don't make yourself cozy in it. Don't indulge your ego at the expense of your soul" (1 Pet 2:11). Home is no longer where we are from, but where we are headed. We don't need to travel to a foreign country to feel like a visitor. We are homeless in our homeland. Peter's word for "foreigner" (παροίκους) literally means "by-dwellers."

After graduating from college, I lived for eight months in Chung Li, Taiwan. I taught a course in world religions and Christian apologetics at a science and engineering college. One day I was summoned to the local police station and questioned. They wanted to know why I had come to their country, what was I doing at the college, and how long I planned on staying. They said they wanted to make sure that I wasn't a "troublemaker." The officers were polite, but they made it clear that they were in charge and that I was a foreign guest in their country.

On a mission trip to Mongolia in early 1990s I was teaching a course in basic Christianity to more than thirty college students. My colleague Dan Lam had obtained official permission to rent a classroom in the cultural center. On the second day two uniformed officers interrupted our class and ordered us to leave the building. They claimed we had no right to be there and that if we did not leave we would be arrested. Dan explained that he had obtained permission and paid for the room, but they insisted, "You have to leave!"

Since we had no place to go, we held class outside. We shivered in freezing temperatures, but we finished our class that day. We never learned who objected to our presence in the building. Neither the Buddhists nor the Communists were pleased that we were there, but Dan sorted it out

---

4. James, *Saint Bernard of Clairvaux*, 41.

with the authorities and we were back in our classroom the next day. It was obvious that we were guests in a foreign country. What wasn't so obvious was that these young believers were becoming foreigners in their native land because of their commitment to Christ.

For the sake of the gospel, Peter wanted the people of God to embrace their foreign residency even in their own homeland. This new identity may be easier to grasp for Mongolian believers than for many Western believers who believe that their culture is nominally Christian. Peter's advice to first-century believers living in Asia Minor fits for twenty-first-century believers living in America. We are resident aliens following a strategy of submission and sacrifice.

THE POLITICS OF SUBMISSION

"Submission" or "subordination" is a key concept in Peter's Christ for culture strategy. He urges believers to be submissive or subordinate in four ways: politically, socially, maritally, and generationally.

> Submit yourselves for the Lord's sake to every human authority . . . (1 Pet 2:13).
>
> Slaves, in reverent fear of God submit yourselves to your masters . . . (1 Pet 2:18).
>
> Wives, in the same way submit yourselves to your husbands . . . (1 Pet 3:1).
>
> The holy women of the past . . . submitted themselves to their own husbands . . .(1 Pet 3:5).
>
> In the same way, you who are younger submit yourselves to your elders (1 Pet 5:5).

Peter acknowledged that the civil authorities have their place in maintaining order and deserve to be respected and obeyed up to a point. But he never implied that the state is owed the believer's emotional "loyalty" or "patriotism." Respectful compliance is not the same as offering praise and commendation. Peter articulated a sober and limited acceptance of the role of the emperor and his governors.[5] At first glance Peter's Christ for culture

---

5. Elliott writes, "On the whole, the Petrine author's view of civil government stands midpoint between the thoroughly positive position of Paul and the entirely negative view of the author of Revelation . . ." Elliott, *1 Peter*, 494.

strategy may look more like a defense of the status quo than a fundamental revolution of the social order. He seems to be advocating a bow-down-and-take-it philosophy, rather than calling for a stand-up-and-take-charge campaign.

Western Christians today don't like to be told to be submissive to anyone—even to those who are legitimately in charge. We feel it is our duty to stand up for ourselves and resist even the appearance of subordination. We live in very different time, politically, economically, and socially. Does this mean that Peter's strategy of submission is anachronistic and belongs in the first century? Is this why 1 Peter tends to be overlooked and neglected? It is true that Caesar is no longer "the supreme authority," wielding his power over civilization, but it is often said that the president of the United States is the most powerful person in the world. He exerts political and economic power over people who didn't vote for him (and Americans like it that way!). We no longer have a slave economy, but as the disparity between the rich and poor widens, many people are practically slaves. Much of what we Americans buy is made in sweatshop conditions overseas. We don't buy and sell human beings in this country, but money still enslaves the human soul, and human trafficking remains a global social problem. Instead of one single supreme authority, we have many dominating authorities ruling over us in business, politics, sports, finance, entertainment, and education. The emperor is no longer running things from Rome, but elites are running things from New York, London, Beijing, and Dubai.

THE POLITICAL ILLUSION

So our world may not be as different from Peter's world as we think. French sociologist and Christian theologian Jacques Ellul lamented that the West suffered from a political illusion. People assume that there is a political solution for everything and that freedom and justice can be obtained by politics. Instead of experiencing real freedom, Ellul argued, people are duped into giving themselves passionately to politics.

"We talk endlessly of politics," he wrote, "in an unconscious effort to hide the void in our actual situation."[6] Political action is a subterfuge diverting attention from the real source of freedom and justice. The French sociologist claimed that our first priority must be "to demythologize politics

---

6. Ellul, *The Political Illusion*, 5.

and put it into its proper, limited place."[7] He rejected the notion that political action and engagement were capable of fundamentally changing the individual and society for the better.

Ellul saw politics as important, but only in a limited way. "My aim is not to invite people to cease being interested in political affairs or to disregard them." But we have to give up the notion that we can control society through political action. "The hope must be surrendered that constitutional rules, good institutions, or socioeconomic changes will modify anything in a decisive fashion. The hope must be abandoned that the citizen will be able to control the state. Politics is a problem of life, and of life without respite. . . . Justice cannot be had in politics."[8]

Ellul reasoned that in a democracy we have to admit "the relatively limited scope of all political debate. To admit this relativity will prevent people from becoming agitated to the point of delirium . . ."[9] He wrote, "It is necessary to help the citizens' political feelings, reactions, and thoughts become less dramatic."[10] Ellul argued that the media in a competitive consumer environment fosters "the arbitrary and illusory world of superficial political judgments and superficial emotional reactions."[11] The citizen becomes "the plaything of orthodoxies" and "easy prey for propaganda."[12] A sure sign of misplaced hope is when believers respond to a political election by throwing up their hands and saying, "This is the end! There's no hope!"

The Apostle Peter and the sociologist Ellul were looking at two radically different political realities (imperial Rome and Western democracies) but their hope in Christ brought them to a similar conclusion. They rejected the political illusion that placed their hope and confidence in their capacity to bring about political and social change. The people of God deserve to hear that message today more than ever. Many believers are unnecessarily agitated and traumatized, some to the point of "delirium," over social hostility. But the culture remains as it has been since the time of Christ, systemically and fundamentally antithetical to the gospel of Jesus Christ.

An inflated understanding of political power and control (Ellul's political illusion) has spawned a web of related illusions that confuse and agitate

7. Ibid., x.
8. Ibid., 202.
9. Ibid., 202–3.
10. Ibid., 203.
11. Ibid.
12. Ibid., 204.

well-meaning believers. Sociologist James Hunter argues that Christians hold naively to the notion that ideas change the world through individuals who sincerely practice their faith. The theory that Christians only need to change "hearts and minds" and work to "get out the vote" in order to change society underestimates the complexity of culture. Culture is a "slow product of history," producing an intricate system of norms and commitments embedded in a confluence of narratives rather than in neatly laid out propositional ideas.[13] Hunter argues that cultural change comes from the top down, not the bottom up, and "rarely if ever without a fight." Hunter concludes, "The work of world-making and world-changing are, by and large, the work of elites: gatekeepers who provide creative direction and management within spheres of social life."[14]

Many Christians who think that they are "on fire for Jesus" have no idea how much they have conformed to this world. Hunter warns, "Most of what really counts, in terms of what shapes us and directs us, we are not aware of; it operates far below what most of us are capable of consciously grasping."[15] We may see ourselves as world changers but in reality we are products of the world. The thin veneer of cultural Christianity is no match for interfacing with the complexity of culture. Even transformed "hearts and minds" are naive in the face of cultural conformity and capitulation. This is why the idolatry of money, sports, sex, and selfish pleasure is such a problem among professing Christians. We are hardly aware of the addictive power these forces have over us. We think we are free but we are not. We are manipulated by media powers, political propaganda, and capitalistic consumerism. Instead of capitulating to cultural pressures, Peter challenges the people of God to accept the gospel's revolutionary strategy. This is how the world's underdog overcomes the world.

> 1. The first step toward an effective and faithful Christ and culture strategy calls for believers to embrace their "foreign" status.
>
> 2. The second step is for them to submit "for the Lord's sake to every human authority" (1 Pet 2:13). This will assure that the gospel revolution is neither politicized nor spiritualized.
>
> 3. The third step calls for them to do good and live free. Peter writes, "For it is God's will that by doing good you should silence

---

13. Hunter, *To Change the World*, 33.
14. Ibid., 43.
15. Ibid., 33.

the ignorant talk of foolish people. Live as free people, but do not use your freedom as a cover-up for evil; live as God's slaves" (1 Pet 2:15–16).

IMPRESSING PAGANS

Peter's spiritual direction is as clear as it is challenging, and impossible apart from the Spirit of Christ. It is guaranteed to draw the ire of the devil. Live such good lives in the public arena that you silence the slander of non-Christians. Turn their accusations into praise. "Live an exemplary life among the natives so that your actions will refute their prejudices" (1 Pet 2:12, *The Message*).

My friend and coworker David Mensah sought to prevent the routine poisoning of the Black Volta in northern Ghana with DDT. For years the fisherman used this lethal insecticide to kill fish. The poisoned fish floated to the surface and the fisherman gathered the dead fish and sold them at market. They didn't realize that they were slowly destroying the environment and their livelihood. With considerable effort, David convinced many of the tribal leaders that DDT would eventually wipe out all the fish. Nearly 500 villagers volunteered to police the river and make sure no one polluted it. Fishermen who violated the ban on DDT were caught and fined.

David's initiative angered some of the fishermen who refused to accept the fact that DDT was destroying the river and their livelihood. A man by the name of Ator became especially vindictive, slandering and insulting David and spreading falsehoods wherever he could. Months passed, the ban on DDT held, and the river slowly came back to life. Nile Perch, which had not been fished on the Black Volta for some time, were now in good supply and the fishermen were happy.

Peter said, "Live such good lives among the pagans that, though they accuse you of doing wrong, they may see your good deeds and glorify God on the day he visits us" (1 Pet 2:12). Remarkably, Ator approached David and asked for forgiveness. "I want your forgiveness," he explained. "I hated you and I took every opportunity to condemn you. But you were right." Confessions like that don't happen very often in this life. Peter implies as much when he refers to the day of God's visitation. We may have to wait until God comes in his glory for pagans to recognize our good work, but this acknowledgment will come eventually.

The freedom of the people of God is not defined by their political or economic or social status but by their relationship to the triune God. To be God's slave means true freedom. As the Apostle Paul said, "It is for freedom that Christ has set us free. Stand firm, then, and do not let yourself be burdened again by a yoke of slavery" (Gal 5:1). "Honor everyone," Peter's simple command, "flattened the status pyramid of the Roman world." He recognized the emperor and the "slave next door" as worthy of respect and honor.[16] And then Peter boldly placed the honor of the emperor in tension with the fear of God. It is not difficult to hear echoes of Peter's defense given before the Sanhedrin years before, when he said, "We must obey God rather than human beings!" (Acts 5:29).

A QUIET REVOLUTION

One of my Christian heroes is John Perkins. You won't find him in the Bible, but you will find the Bible in John Perkins. In college, I read his story, *A Quiet Revolution*. He describes the night he was brutally beaten by the police in Brandon, Mississippi, after participating in a nonviolent civil rights march.

> During my night in the jail at Brandon, God began something new in my life. In the midst of the crowded, noisy jailhouse, between the stomping and the blackjacking that we received; between the moments when one of the patrolmen put his pistol to my head and pulled the trigger—"click"—and when another later took a fork and bent the two middle prongs down and pushed the other two up my nose until blood came out—between the reality and the insanity, between the consciousness and the unconsciousness that would sweep across my dizzy mind, between my terror and my unwillingness to break down, between my pain and my fear, in those little snatches of thought when in some miraculous way I could at once be the spectacle and the spectator, God pushed me past hatred. Just for a little while, moments at a time.
>
> How could I hate when there was so much to pity? How could I hate people I suddenly did not recognize, who had somehow moved past the outer limits of what it means to be human? But I don't think it was just the pity I had or the deep sickness I saw alone that pushed me past hatred. It was also the fact that I was broken.... The Brandon experience just might have been a way of

---

16. Green, *1 Peter*, 76.

> God bringing me to the place where he could expand his love in me and extend my calling to white people as well as black people. ... And I believe that it was in my own broken state that the depth of the sickness in those men struck home to me, and the fact that I was like them—totally depraved. I had evidence before me and in myself that every human being is bad—depraved. There's something built into all of us that makes us want to be superior. If the black man had the advantage, he'd be just as bad. So I can't hate the white man. It's a spiritual problem—black or white, we all need to be born again ... .[17]

John Perkins found God's severe mercy in a Brandon city jail pushing him past hate to love and forgiveness. Human evil was an instrument in the hands of his loving heavenly Father used to transform raw evil into divine goodness. No matter how deep the depravity or painful the social alienation, there is room at the table of the Lord in the household of faith. In a world of evil and hostility, the gospel of Jesus Christ is an inclusive invitation to an exclusive Savior and Lord. We come as we are but we do not remain as we were. We are new creations created in Christ Jesus. We have a new citizenship, a new family, and an entirely new indwelling Spirit.

"The gospel of Jesus Christ is more political than anyone imagines, but in a way that no one guesses."[18] The inside-out revolution empowered by the gospel is always *personal* before it is *political*, always *relational* before it is *institutional*, always *spiritual* before it is *social*. Beatitude-based believers are salt and light disciples—God's workmanship created in Christ Jesus to do good works. We are called to work out our "salvation with fear and trembling, for it is God who works in [us] to will and act in order to fulfill his good purpose" (Phil 2:12–13). Those who know Christ personally cannot help but have a social impact.

Jesus commanded us to love our neighbor as ourselves and then he redefined the "neighbor" to include those we were least likely to like, let alone love. Such love is bound to have a social impact. He taught us to pray, "Our Father in heaven, hallowed be your name, your kingdom come, your will be done on earth as it is in heaven" (Matt 6:9–10). To pray this way we cannot help but trust in God to reveal his goodness. He commissioned his followers, "Go and make disciples of all nations, baptizing them in the name of the Father and of the Son and of the Holy Spirit, and teaching them to obey everything I have commanded you" (Matt 28:19–20). Such

17. Perkins, *A Quiet Revolution*, 190–91.
18. Peterson, *Reversed Thunder*, 117.

obedience cannot help but have a social impact. If we seek Christ first, before his kingdom, we will draw people to Christ. "Every movement we make in response to God has a ripple effect, touching family, neighbors, friends, community."[19]

Peter makes a strong case for the faithfulness of God. We are chosen "according to the foreknowledge of God the Father, through the sanctifying work of the Spirit, because of the obedience of Jesus Christ and the sprinkling of his blood" (1 Pet 1:2). We are given new birth into a living hope, blessed with a lasting inheritance, and shielded by the power of God until the coming of salvation. We are redeemed by the precious blood of Christ. God pursues us, identifies with us, and offers us life by his sacrificial love.

James Hunter's sociology dovetails beautifully with the message of 1 Peter. The people of God are called and empowered to establish a faithful presence. Their aim is not to change the world but to be changed by Christ in the world. Hunter writes, "A theology of faithful presence is a theology of engagement in and with the world around us. It is a theology of commitment, a theology of promise. It is disarmingly simple in concept yet in its implications it provides a challenge, at points, to all of the dominant paradigms of cultural engagement in the church."[20]

---

19. Peterson, *The Message Remix*, 1412.
20. Hunter, *To Change the World*, 242–43.

6

God's Slaves

Slaves, in reverent fear of God submit yourselves to your masters, not only to those who are good and considerate, but also to those who are harsh. For it is commendable if someone bears up under the pain of unjust suffering because he or she is conscious of God. But how is it to your credit if you receive a beating for doing wrong and you endure it? But if you suffer for doing good and you endure it, this is commendable before God.

To this you were called, because Christ suffered for you, leaving you an example, that you should follow in his steps. "He committed no sin, and no deceit was found in his mouth." When they hurled their insults at him, he did not retaliate; when he suffered, he made no threats. Instead, he entrusted himself to him who judges justly. "He himself bore our sins" in his body on the cross, so that we might die to sins and live for righteousness; "by his wounds you have been healed." For "you were like sheep going astray," but now you have returned to the Shepherd and Overseer of your souls. 1 Peter 2:18–25

We should not be surprised that the apostles who turned the world upside down gave us a bottom-up profile of the disciple. If you want to know how to live for Christ in a pagan culture, look to the worker who has a harsh boss or to the woman who has a difficult husband or to the teenager who is ridiculed by her peers at school. Peter's bottom-up examples of Christlike maturity set the stage for his Christ for culture strategy.

Outposts of Hope

When my seminary students read James Hunter's *To Change the World* they expect him to challenge Christians to aspire for positions of influence. Hunter makes a strong case for top-down cultural change. Networks of elites produce the greatest impact on cultural change. Students anticipate an evangelical charge to take back these strategic centers, to graduate from Ivy League schools, to head for the corporate corner office, to campaign for political office, and to be all that they can be to change the world.

But Hunter throws them a curve. He challenges the triumphal dreaming and guilt-inducing blame that claims the world is as bad as it is because Christians have failed to grasp the reins of power. Hunter holds out little hope for changing the world from the top down or from the bottom up. The world is the world and the world will be the world until Christ comes again. New Testament Christianity is not calling Christians to aspire to cultural greatness or join the ranks of the elite or take back America in a groundswell of populist support. Hunter argues that "a disposition and relationality of superiority, condescension, and entitlement by social elites" is "abhorrent for the Christian." "By its very nature, elitism is exploitative. So far as I can tell, elitism for believers is despicable and utterly anathema to the gospel they cherish."[1]

> The worst possible conclusion, then, is that what Christians need is a new strategy for achieving and holding on to power in the world—at least in any conventional sense. Such a conclusion is not only wrong on its own terms, it is wrong because Christians operate with an understanding of power that is derived from the larger and dominant culture of the late modern world.[2]

First Peter challenges the prevailing popular evangelical strategies for engaging culture. Instead of looking at the culturally elite for inspiration, Peter looked at the culturally despised for models of true faithfulness. He found his examples among subjects, slaves, and women. He wanted Christ's followers to remember that they were resident aliens, foreigners, and strangers in a pagan culture.[3] His purpose was to encourage them to follow the incarnational model of the Master.

---

1. Hunter, *To Change the World*, 94.
2. Ibid., 99–100.
3. Hunter writes, "Faithful presence in practice is the exercise of leadership in all spheres and all levels of life and activity. It represents a quality of commitment oriented to the fruitfulness, wholeness, and well-being of all. It is therefore the opposite of elitism and the domination it implies. It is also the antithesis of celebrity, a model of leadership

God's Slaves

THE HOUSEHOLD CODE

Greco-Roman culture had a long tradition of moral instruction for the household, the basic social unit of society. Plato, Aristotle, and Seneca all weighed in on how masters and slaves, husbands and wives, parents and children ought to behave toward one another. Moral order in the household was the basis for "a strong, orderly, and prosperous society."[4] Peter's focus on these relationships silenced the charge that Christ's followers were indifferent to social harmony and moral order. Peter set out to prove that Christians were model subjects, obedient slaves, and respectful spouses, but the source for his moral instruction was not Greek philosophy but the Old Testament. The gospel's quiet revolution was based on goodness, not conflict. Peter began at the bottom rung of the social ladder to work out the practical reality of the gospel. To begin here turned everything upside down in a way uniquely related to Jesus Christ's incarnational descent.

Peter neither talks down to slaves nor does he talk about slaves; he talks to slaves. He affords them personal respect: "You household slaves." The word he used for "slave" was οἰκέται, meaning household slave (the word belongs to the οἰκία word group). It is a different word than the one he used when he said, "live as God's slaves." There he used the familiar δοῦλος. This is important, because before he personally addresses "household slaves" he calls *all* Christ-followers *God's slaves*. Peter's perspective harmonizes well with Paul's extensive use of the word δοῦλος.

Like Paul, Peter stayed with the title "slave of Christ" or "God's slave." He shared Paul's redefined meaning of "slave" in the light of the gospel. Our relationship with Christ takes precedence over our social standing. Slaves are free in Christ and those who are free should consider themselves Christ's slaves. Peter and Paul shared a common understanding and usage of the slave imagery. It is reasonable to assume that Peter echoed Paul's word to the Galatians? "Am I now trying to win human approval, or God's approval? Or am I trying to please people? If I were still trying to please people, I would not be a slave (δοῦλος) of Christ" (Gal 1:10). Peter's distinction between "God's slaves" and "household servants" fits with Paul's description: "Though I am free and belong to no one, I have made myself a slave to everyone, to win as many as possible" (1 Cor 9:19). Peter would

---

that many Christians in prominent positions have a very difficult time resisting. Celebrity is, in effect, based on an inflated brilliance, accomplishment, or spirituality generated and perpetuated by publicity. It is an artifice and, therefore, a type of fraud." Ibid., 260.

4. Jobes, *1 Peter*, 181.

have agreed with Paul's charge to believers not to use their freedom to indulge their sinful nature, but "to be slaves (δουλεύετε) to one another in love" (Gal 5:13). Paul's encouragement to believers in Corinth only serves to support Peter's spiritual direction:

> Keeping God's commands is what counts. Each of you should remain in the situation you were in when God called you. Were you a slave when you were called? Don't let it trouble you—although if you can gain your freedom, do so. For those who were slaves when called to faith in the Lord are the Lord's freed people; similarly, those who were free when called are Christ's slaves. You were bought at a price; do not become slaves of human beings. Brothers and sisters, all of you, as responsible to God, should remain in the situation in which God called you (1 Cor 7:19–14).

In first-century–Greco-Roman culture, slavery was the social, legal, and economic reality. It was not subject to debate. Slavery was central to the economic order as our "service industry" is to our economy. "The institution of slavery was a fact of Mediterranean economic life so completely accepted as a part of the labor structure of the time that one cannot correctly speak of the slave 'problem' in antiquity."[5] In Peter's day, one-third of the population of Greece and Italy were slaves. The Roman Senate debated whether or not to require slaves to wear identifying clothing, but they decided against uniforms for fear that the slave population would realize how large and potentially powerful they were.

Unlike American slavery, slaves in the ancient Greco-Roman world were not drawn from one race, nor were their duties limited to manual labor. Slaves were responsible for a broad range of economic activities, including administrative positions in the household of the emperor, civil service jobs, medical care, teaching, accountancy, business enterprises, and domestic and agricultural work. Some slaves lived very well, with a higher status and standard of living than free people. Some people sold themselves into slavery "in order to climb socially, to obtain particular employment open only to slaves, and to enjoy a better standard of living than they had experienced as free persons. Being a slave had the benefit of providing a certain personal and social security."[6] However, slavery under any circumstances is dehumanizing. The Oscar-winning movie *Gladiator*, starring Russell Crowe, tells the story of Maximus, a Roman general who is betrayed

---

5. Lincoln, *Ephesians*, 415.
6. Ibid., 418.

and sold into slavery. The movie offers a realistic picture of the brutality and humiliation of slavery in first-century Rome.

Instead of feeling inferior, slaves were meant to experience real freedom in Christ. The old criteria of social standing based on ethnicity, religion, and social class no longer controlled the believer's identity, self-worth, and fulfillment. Far from rendering believers passive to social pressures, Peter sought to make them immune to social pressures. "Believers are not to return to the bondage of an honor-shame culture where everything revolves round what status is achieved in human eyes."[7]

Ultimately the only freedom worth having is the freedom found in Christ, because only that freedom sets us free from the selfish social values of the world, from the dog-eat-dog world of cutthroat competition, and from the law of sin and death.

SPIRITUAL DIRECTION

Peter addressed household slaves as key members in the household of God.[8] The servant who "bears up under the pain of unjust suffering because he or she is conscious of God" is held up as the model for all believers (1 Pet 2:19). Peter was eager to use the slave to exemplify Christ. For both Peter and Paul Christian slaves were called to illustrate the cost of discipleship. Consider the following:

> 1. By addressing slaves directly as full-fledged members of the body of Christ, Peter dignified the slave as a brother or sister in Christ with equal standing before the Lord. Relationships among brothers and sisters in Christ "embody their Lord's ultimate disregard for any distinctions based on social status."[9]

> 2. The apostles applied the gospel to everyday life. They emphasized the sanctity and sacrifice of work as a holy calling. Even the dark side of a difficult employment situation was part of God's call. "To this you were called," Peter wrote, "because Christ suffered for

---

7. Thiselton, *The First Epistle to the Corinthians*, 562.

8. Joel Green writes, "Given the nature of slavery as an institutionalized form of marginality and Peter's characterization of his audience as people who, because of their loyalty to Jesus, inhabit the outer perimeters of honorable society, it is easy to find in vv. 18–20 an address to all Christians rather than to a subset. The presence of 'slave' and 'household slave' side-by-side would signal Peter's instruction applies to all who comprise the 'household of God.'" Green, *1 Peter*, 77–78.

9. Lincoln, *Ephesians*, 428.

you, leaving you an example, that you should follow in his steps" (1 Pet 2:21).

3. Implicit in this description is Peter's assurance that the obedience of a household slave was on par with his own. Their calling was no different from his own. Their obedience was "paradigmatic of the entire community; their suffering with the suffering of the innocent Christ (1 Pet 2:21–24) is that of all innocent believers who share in this suffering (1 Pet 4:1,13).

4. Peter encouraged slaves to focus on their reverent fear of God and to remain conscious of God in spite of suffering unjustly. They were to associate their unjust suffering with Christ's suffering. It is not difficult to see how Christ's followers stuck in difficult employment situations today might apply Peter's spiritual direction.

Household slaves who took Peter's counsel to heart may have had an advantage over believers today. We think we are in control of our lives, but they knew better. We talk big about freedom but we are slaves to money and debt, technologies and schedules, lusts and leisure. We have our hidden bondage to contend with.

We think we are what we do and what we own, but they knew better. In Christ, these household slaves had an identity beyond the drudgery of work. They refused to confuse their job with their self-worth.

We think we want our neighbor's life, but they knew better. We covet his car, her clothes, his job, her fun, his reputation, her success, but slaves were required to give themselves away. They rejected the temptation to turn things and people into "immortality symbols." They did not have the luxury of contemplating the American myth that says you can be anything you want to be.

We think our lives should be easier, but they knew better. They knew life was brutally hard and they accepted it with grace and patience.

We think we need to make a difference with our lives, but they knew better. They were slaves; their lives could not be defined by results and achievements. Meaning and significance had to be found in Christ and in obedience.

We think we can solve our problems by moving away, switching churches, changing jobs, but they knew better. They couldn't leave; they had to stay. They had to live for Christ under conditions and circumstances that they had little control over.

We think that friendships should enrich our lives and give us something in return, but they knew better. Slaves of Christ befriend fellow strugglers not for what they can get out of the relationship, but for what they can give.

When I consider Peter's spiritual direction, I think of David, a Christian teenager who stocks shelves and bags groceries at a large supermarket. He worked at the grocery store all through high school. He loves working there now so much that when he comes home from college they always fit him into the schedule. "But it wasn't always that way," he explained.

> I used to hate the work. I found it totally demoralizing. I felt like I was everybody's servant. I literally despised it, but I needed the money. Then one day, when I was in a particularly bad mood, a customer calmly said to me, "You don't like working here, do you?" The comment really upset me. I didn't think people picked up on my bad attitude or if they did, that it mattered much. But that little comment hit me like a ton of bricks, because I knew that a Christian shouldn't go around acting mad all the time. So, I got serious with the Lord. I confessed my terrible work ethic and prayed for strength to change my attitude. The change was remarkable. I realized that my job was not just about bagging groceries and stocking shelves but it was about serving Christ. I went from hating my job to loving it. I used to run from people, hide from my boss, and do as little work as possible. Now I enjoy the people, respect my boss, and do as much work as I can get done. Back in my bad attitude days my shift seemed to last forever and I couldn't wait to get out of there, but now things are different. Somebody the other day said to me, "You like to work here, don't you?"

THE SUFFERING SERVANT

The only New Testament passage that "explicitly and extensively" links Jesus and Isaiah's description of the Suffering Servant is the one that links Jesus' suffering with the unjust suffering of Christian slaves.[10] Peter did not hesitate to parallel the atoning sacrifice of Christ with the suffering of believers, even though such "suffering does not appear in pagan household codes and is unique to Peter's purposes."[11] Only Peter gives us a Suffering

---

10. Jobes, *1 Peter*, 187.
11. Ibid., 191.

Servant Christology that applies the doctrine of the atonement to how Christians should be willing to suffer unjustly.

Christ is our example (ὑπογραμμὸν). Peter used a Greek word popular in early childhood education that referred to how children learn to write by tracing letters. Picture Isaiah's Suffering Servant, Jesus, with his hand upon your hand, guiding your hand as you trace the letters. That is Peter's image. "English words such as 'example,' 'model,' or 'pattern' are too weak," writes Karen Jobes, "for Jesus' suffering is not simply an example or pattern or model, as if one of many; he is *the* paradigm by which Christians write large the letters of his gospel in their lives."[12] Following in Christ's footsteps conveys an image of intimacy and immediacy. The very one who "committed no sin" (1 Pet 2:22) uttered no insult, and refused to retaliate, is right there with the believer leading the way. But then, Peter takes the example of Christ to an even deeper level. Not only is Christ our model for unjust suffering, but Christ suffered unjustly *for us*, because of our sin. "He himself bore our sins in his body on the tree" (1 Pet 2:24). He took upon himself our sin and death "so that we might die to sins and live for righteousness; 'by his wounds you have been healed'" (1 Pet 2:24). The vicarious atoning sacrifice of Christ on the cross is the bedrock foundation for the messianic community's relationship to culture. Whatever suffering we experience because of the gospel must be seen in the light of Christ's atoning sacrifice *for us*. Peter closes with a pastoral image of comfort and protection: "For 'you were like sheep going astray,' but now you have returned to the Shepherd and Overseer of your souls" (1 Pet 2:25).

UNJUST SUFFERING

It is scandalous that the one who healed the sick, loved the outcast, and transformed the sinner should die a hideously cruel death by Roman crucifixion. What kind of world do we live in that sentences holy and compassionate men and women to die? Jesus exposes the fact that the political and religious authorities are not always on the side of righteousness. Greed, pride, and hate often control the power brokers of society. Jesus became a victim for the sake of righteousness. It was impossible for anyone living in the first century to gloss over the practical social consequences of following Jesus. The cross made sure of that. Early Christians knew that their lives were marked by the cross, but today many Christians give the impression

---

12. Ibid., 195.

that a decision for Jesus simply involves submitting mentally to the idea that Jesus died for their sins.

On the other hand, those who wish to emphasize the political side of Jesus' death tend to ignore the evidence of the Gospels. Jesus' message had political impact, but it was completely different from the political impact of the Zealots. Jesus resisted violence (Luke 9:54–55; John 18:10–11), rejected popular support (John 2:24; 6:15), and flatly denied that his kingdom was of the world (John 18:36). He neither defended the status quo nor encouraged revolution. He refused to be tricked into nationalism. He insisted on God's authority over all of life, without making a secular-spiritual dichotomy (Mark 12:17; John 19:11). He narrowed his loyal supporters down to a small band of men and women but right up to the end remained accessible to the public through his daily teaching (Mark 14:48–49). The meaning of his life simply cannot be exhausted politically. Although his death has tremendous political significance, he lived and died for something far more significant than a political cause. This truth is part of the confusion and the tragedy of the cross. From a political point of view Jesus did not have to die. It is true that the Jewish Sanhedrin feared for its social privilege and political influence, but this fear alone was not sufficient to account for his death (John 11:48). To contend that Jesus' strategy of nonviolence and his condemnation of those who wielded the sword resulted in the death penalty goes beyond the evidence. It is difficult to support the conclusion that Jesus was a greater political threat than Barabbas. John Yoder exaggerated when he wrote: "His alternative was so relevant, so much a threat, that Pilate could afford to free, in exchange for Jesus, the ordinary Guevara type insurrectionist Barabbas."[13]

The Gospels do not develop the political impact of Jesus sufficiently to lead logically and inevitably to the cross. This inability to explain Jesus' death simply in political terms is part of the frustration and despair of the cross. Pilate did not have to kill Jesus. Nowhere is it suggested that he considered Jesus a greater threat to Roman rule than Barabbas. If anything, he probably released Barabbas and sentenced Jesus only to pacify the Jews. His judgment was not decided because he feared the political impact of Jesus' civil disobedience. In all likelihood, much of what Jesus said and did escaped Pilate's notice. The death of Jesus was a relatively small matter for Pilate. Politically speaking, Jesus could have walked away a free man instead of being nailed to the cross. Part of the scandal of the cross is that

---

13. Yoder, *The Politics of Jesus*, 112.

God's purposes are accomplished and his word is fulfilled in the midst of political ambiguity and seemingly accidental circumstances.

A PASSION NARRATIVE

As a thirteen-year-old I was troubled by the death of Dr. Paul Carlson, a medical missionary in the Republic of Congo. Carlson had been falsely accused by the rebel Simbas of being a major in the American military, a mercenary instead of a missionary doctor. On November 24, 1964, as Belgium paratroopers were landing in Stanleyville, Carlson, along with a number of other hostages, was led by Simba guards out into the middle of the street while guns were firing all around the area. In the mad confusion some of the hostages were hit in the cross fire. Some ran for the nearest protection. A small group ran to the shelter of a house and clambered over the porch wall. One of the hostages leaped over the wall and reached back. He had his fingers on Paul's sweater when a young Simba came around the corner and fired off five shots, instantly killing Paul Carlson. A second or two later and he would have been on the other side of the wall. His body was graphically shown throughout the world on the glossy pages of *Life* magazine.

At the time, he seemed to me more a victim of tragic circumstances than an ambassador for Christ who gave his life for the gospel. Since then, I have come to see that the Christian's cross, like Jesus' cross, must be interpreted on two levels. On the one level, confusion and ambiguity surround the meaning and interpretation of our lives. From this perspective, Dr. Carlson's death was nothing more than meaningless circumstances leading to a tragedy that might easily have been averted. But what may appear to be a tragic, accidental moment is in fact an orchestrated movement in the sovereign plan of God. In so many ways, Paul Carlson died like his Lord.

On the one hand, Jesus appears as the victim of circumstances—a friend betrays him, popular sentiment turns against him, a ruler concerned only with political expediency hears his case, and his disciples abandon him. But on the other hand, Jesus dies (in accord with Old Testament prophecy) as the lamb who was slain from the foundation of the world (Luke 24:25-27; 1 Pet 1:20; Rev 13:8). There is an inevitability about his death that lies outside historical circumstances and human arrangements. It is impossible to adequately understand the suffering and death of Jesus apart from God's interpretation of the event. God infuses the cross with meaning from three primary sources: the history of God's revelation to Israel, Jesus' self-disclosure, and the apostolic witness. There is a tremendous redemptive purpose arising out of the muddle of historical circumstances. This glorious purpose is not the product of human imagination and wishful thinking. It is the fulfillment of God's eternal plan of redemption. The real scandal of the cross lies in the fact that God in Christ, the Savior of the world, was crucified.

Four months before Paul Carlson died he delivered a message in Lingala at the Wasolo Regional Church Conference. His message was from 1 Peter 2:21–24:

> To this you were called, because Christ suffered for you, leaving you an example, that you should follow in his steps. . . . He himself bore our sins in his body on the tree, so that we might die to sins and live for righteousness; by his wounds you have been healed.

"At this conference," Paul began, "we are going to think about following Jesus. It is not hard to follow Jesus when all goes well, but sometimes it is difficult to follow Him when the road is difficult." After he described the state of persecution for Christ's sake in various regions in the Congo, he said, "We do not know what will happen in 1964, until we meet together again. We do not know if we will suffer or die during this year because we are Christians. But it does not matter! Our job is to follow Jesus."[14]

Carlson went on to describe briefly, in simple New Testament logic, the persecution experienced by the early church. "How does all of this apply to us at Wasolo?" Paul asked. "Jesus is asking us if we are willing to suffer for Him. This is of the greatest importance to all of us Christians here today." Then Paul introduced the sacrament of holy communion. He said,

> We are going to gather together at the Lord's Table. Before taking part, I think each person should ask themselves if they are willing to suffer for Jesus Christ if need be—and if he or she is willing even to die if necessary—during this coming year. Taking part in Communion means union with Jesus. Union with Jesus sometimes means joy—but union with Jesus sometimes means suffering. My friends, if today you are not willing to suffer for Jesus, do not partake of the elements. If you do take the cup and bread here today, be certain that you are willing to give your life for Jesus during 1964 or 1965 if it is necessary. To follow Jesus means to be willing to suffer for Him. Will you follow Jesus this year?[15]

14. Carlson, *Monganga Paul*, 129.
15. Ibid., 130.

Within two months many of the Congolese believers who heard this message and participated in holy communion that day suffered persecution unto death for Christ's sake. They, along with Paul Carlson, leave a testimony that inspires and challenges our faithfulness for Christ and his kingdom.

7

Mutual Love

Wives, in the same way submit yourselves to your own husbands so that, if any of them do not believe the word, they may be won over without words by the purity and reverence of your lives. Your beauty should not come from outward adornment, such as elaborate hairstyles and the wearing of gold jewelry or fine clothes. Rather, it should be that of your inner self, the unfading beauty of a gentle and quiet spirit, which is of great worth in God's sight. For this is the way the holy women of the past who put their hope in God used to adorn themselves. They submitted themselves to their own husbands, like Sarah, who obeyed Abraham and called him her lord. You are her daughters if you do what is right and do not give way to fear.

Husbands, in the same way be considerate as you live with your wives, and treat them with respect as the weaker partner and as heirs with you of the gracious gift of life, so that nothing will hinder your prayers. 1 Peter 3:1–7

The Lord's work of transformation began in Jean's life several years before a jet ski accident claimed the life of her ten-year-old son, Tom. Five months prior to the accident she and her husband finalized their divorce. For Jean it was a perfect storm. In her battle with alcoholism, she had been sober for two and a half years prior to Tom's death. She held onto her sobriety with all her might, not only to honor her son's life, but knowing that getting sober again, if she "fell off the wagon," might not happen.

Up to this point she had not publicly acknowledged the Lord's help in her life, but she knew the Lord was at work in her. Ten days after Tom's funeral, Jean's Christian women friends, some of whom she played beach volleyball with, whisked her into a Bible study on Romans. "I invited Jesus into my heart at that time," says Jean, "although as a youngster I had walked with him." Jean fit the Apostle Peter's description: she was chosen according to the foreknowledge of God the Father, through the sanctifying work of the Spirit, because of the obedience of Jesus Christ and the sprinkling of his blood (1 Pet 1:2).

Otis and Jean met over beach volleyball. They had been good friends for fifteen years and they started dating a year after Tom's death. One of her trusted Christian mentors warned her about marrying a non-Christian, but after four years of dating Otis, Jean went ahead anyway, because "Otis was basically so good." A former Marine, Otis was laid back and fun to be with. In all the right ways, he loved and encouraged Jean, but when it came to Christ, she was on her own.

Four years after they were married, Otis was diagnosed with cancer in his face and neck. The prospect of life-threatening surgery on his parotid gland confronted him with an overwhelming sense of his powerlessness. The night before his surgery Jean asked if she could read the Bible to him to comfort them both. He agreed, adding that if he didn't make it through the surgery he would find a place for the two of them in heaven and he would be waiting for her. Jean recalls that she boldly told him that he would not be in heaven! They were heading in different directions! Otis asked how he could have the assurance of his salvation and Jean shared with him the story of Jesus Christ and his gospel. That night, Otis accepted Christ. The surgery was successful and Otis recovered, but he wasn't very interested in joining Jean at church. Jean was careful not to pressure and prod, but she did draw Otis into her morning devotions. The daily times of Bible reading and prayer became a natural extension of their love and marriage.

On the rare occasion when Otis joined Jean at church they would sit in the very last row of the balcony, as far away from the pastor as possible. Then one afternoon Jean invited a family from the church over for a Sunday afternoon barbeque. In the course of conversation, Maddie, only a child at the time, innocently asked why she didn't see Otis at church "every" Sunday. She offered to make it "safe" for Otis to come to church by saving him a seat right next to her. As Jean says, "the rest is history," and indeed the story goes on from there in beautiful ways of witness and worship. Otis came, as

Peter would say, to the Living Stone and became a living stone, "built into a spiritual house to be a holy priesthood, offering spiritual sacrifices acceptable to God through Jesus Christ" (1 Pet 2:4–5).

Jean may be the kind of wife Peter had in mind when he wrote about unbelieving husbands: "If any of them do not believe the word, they may be won over without words by the behavior of their wives" (1 Pet 3:1). You would have to know Jean personally to know how this formerly crazy party girl who had suffered deeplyhm shared her life in Christ quietly and gently, without a hint of pressure or self-righteousness.

PASTORAL PERSPECTIVE

Theologians are inclined to think in broad, abstract terms about big issues. They leave the personal and practical concerns to pastors. They focus on big issues, such as creation care, ecumenism, and politics. They call for social justice on behalf of the poor and the unborn. They discuss church growth trends and urban church planting. They tackle the challenge of pastoral and missionary preparation and analyze various competing world views. All of these issues are important, but Peter did something different from what Christian thinkers tend to do. His spiritual direction focused on the person in community. He wrote from Rome with pastoral purpose and practicality. His recipients were spread out over a vast region, populated by many diverse people groups, but his exhortation and encouragement centered on the personal cost of discipleship. Instead of world-changing abstractions he called for personal sacrifice on the human plane of daily living.

"Dear friends" introduces Peter's first-person Christ for culture strategy. He spoke directly to the people who were responsible for representing Christ at the grassroots. He addressed subjects, slaves, wives, and husbands on the practical meaning of following the crucified Christ. It was not his intention to wrestle with the diversity that swirled around these first-century believers. The world's pluralism was not Peter's concern nor did it set his agenda. His aim was to encourage believers as "foreigners and exiles" to "live such good lives among the pagans" that the world would see the goodness of God (1 Pet 2:12). God's "chosen outsiders" may have felt homeless in the culture, but they were at home in the household of God and they were commissioned to go and make disciples.

In the first two cultural categories, subjects and slaves, the modern reader negotiates the cultural differences relatively easily. The political and economic differences between the first and twenty-first centuries are great, but the meaning of Christlike submission remains understandable. We respect the political authorities, even if it means going to jail because we must obey God, not man. We respect our employer, even if it means suffering unjustly. The world has nothing to fear from Christians other than the demonstration of God's goodness. We will not fight the world with the weapons of the world.

The third category, wives and husbands, is more problematic, because some Christians are unwilling to admit that they live in a very different cultural time. They are okay with political and economic changes, but when it comes to gender stratification they insist nothing has changed, because God has ordained that men should rule and women should follow. They may no longer believe in the divine right of kings or misconstrue the Bible to mandate racial segregation, but they believe that women must be led by men. They credit the gospel of Jesus Christ for leading to democracy and racial equality, but they draw the line at gender mutuality. Instead of reading 1 Peter in the light of ancient patriarchalism and transposing its spiritual direction into our times, they insist on imposing divine sanction on gender stratification and roles. Thankfully, the false acceptance of the "the unalterable 'given-ness' of slavery" and "the 'natural' inferiority of females" has been lifted from modern culture, due in no small measure to the gospel of Jesus Christ.[1] Nevertheless a soft patriarchy persists in spite of the Bible's emphasis on mutuality.

In all three spheres of life—political, social, and familial—Peter lays down the principle of the cross: "my life for yours." Regardless of the governing political, social, and gender ideologies, Peter attacks the world's principle, "your life for mine." Peter refuses to fight culture at the ideological level, partly because of the utter futility of trying to change the human condition from the top down. He attacks it at the personal, practical level. He has nothing more to offer than street-level theology and kitchen-table spiritual direction. But that is what gives his spirituality social impact, whether the government is a democracy or dictatorship; whether the economy is slave-based or capitalistic; whether society is patriarchal or egalitarian. Peter's social theory is not a product of his times; it is the fruit of the gospel of Christ.

Over time the strategy of the gospel changes families from the inside out. Relationships in the household of faith are based on the transforming

---

1. Elliott, *1 Peter*, 589.

work of the Spirit of Christ. The defensive, competitive, manipulative, and domineering relational strategies of the old nature give way to mutual submission and gift-based, every-member ministry in Christ. The church is no longer bound, but free from patriarchal and matriarchal control. Nothing the world has to offer, from traditional male headship to radical feminism, comes close to expressing the new relational dynamic created in Christ Jesus.

If Peter were writing today he might begin this section by offering spiritual direction specifically to singles ("You singles"). Even if Peter did not identify singles as such, it is clear from his letter that a single person in Christ can be truly complete and joyfully whole. Singleness expressed in Christ-centered wholeness is a powerful testimony to the grace and peace of Christ. We know that the Apostle Paul was not reticent about advocating singleness for the sake of the gospel (1 Cor 7). The apostles challenged the false recipe for Christian happiness that many hold dear: falling in love, sexual intimacy in marriage, a successful career, and healthy, well-adjusted children. If the apostles were around today, they might say that perspective looks suspiciously like the American Dream, not the Sermon on the Mount. The message of the gospel is that the single person in Christ can be fully complete and truly whole—a powerful testimony to being chosen, sanctified, and redeemed by the triune God. Humility frees the single person to enjoy life to the fullest.

"YOU WIVES"

Believing wives married to unbelieving husbands were living in an incredibly precarious and vulnerable relationship in first-century Asia Minor. For a wife not to comply with her husband's religion was tantamount to rebellion. Like the slave, she was a powerful picture of the vulnerability of the entire believing community. It is important to note that the contrast is between a slave's harsh master and a wife's unbelieving husband, not an abusive husband. Peter does not condone an abusive husband. Violence in the home is a form of marital unfaithfulness that cannot be excused under any conditions. Spousal abuse was condemned by Greco-Roman legal statutes and "a woman who endured domestic violence would not necessarily have been considered a virtuous wife."[2] Those who "would decry 1 Peter as a piece of deplorable propaganda unworthy of the gospel" seriously

2. Jobes, *1 Peter*, 206.

misconstrue "the aim of the letter, which is not to encourage conformity to secular society but precisely the opposite: to affirm the holiness and distinctiveness of the reborn family of God and to urge holy nonconformity with Gentile modes of thought and life."[3]

Peter's direct address to the believing wife supercedes the controlling opinion of the unbelieving husband and respects the wife's moral responsibility to live for Christ. "In a masterful move, Peter boldly upholds and subverts the social order."[4] He calls for wives to win over their husbands by their behavior, by the purity and reverence of their lives. They are to cultivate the inner beauty of character rather than rely on the superficial beauty of sexual attraction. Peter says in effect, "What matters is not your outer appearance—the styling of your hair, the jewelry you wear, the cut of your clothes—but your inner disposition" (1 Pet 3:3, *The Message*).

Women are under constant pressure in our culture to prove themselves physically attractive. Recently a friend was in the checkout line at the grocery with his wife. He was glancing at the magazines when his eye caught the cover of *Vogue*. He focused for a moment on the bikini-clad model before intentionally averting his eyes. His wife, who had observed his reaction, walked over to the magazine rack, picked up a copy of *Vogue*, pointed to the model, and said, "I can't compete with that!"

This can be an especially hard and competitive culture on women. It is both ironic and embarrassing that our culture tends to measure a woman's worth by her measurements. We have fixated on weight rather than worth and sex appeal rather than character. The less a woman weighs the greater her value and the more she attends to her physical appearance the more attention she receives. I know a person who recently turned down a job in a wealthy suburb of Dallas. One of the considerations that he and his wife discussed was the culture of intimidation generated by women who spend lavishly on clothes and cosmetics and worry incessantly about their weight. Having lived in an upscale culture before, his wife was reluctant to reenter the image wars and battle feelings of inferiority.

Peter's spiritual direction is rooted in an Old Testament theology of beauty. His concern for the inner self, "the unfading beauty of a gentle and quiet spirit" (1 Pet 3:4), reflects a biblical understanding of beauty. In the Old Testament, loveliness was not contained in an object to look at, as in

---

3. Elliott, *1 Peter*, 596–97. Elliot provides an excellent response to Elizabeth Schüssler Fiorenza and Kathleen E. Corley.

4. Jobes, *1 Peter*, 204.

a statue or a painting or magazine cover, but experienced relationally in a picture of wholeness ordained in the created order. William Dyrness explains, "Beauty is only the splendor of a system of relationships; it is an aspect of the totality of meaning of the created order, which for God's people was immediately evident in the whole and in the art."[5]

Biblical aesthetics and the Greek view of art parted company. "In the Old Testament an object or event [or person] is not beautiful because it conforms to a formal ideal but because it reflects in its small way the wholeness of the created order. Sometimes it is lovely if it displays the integrity that characterizes creation and that in turn reflects God's own righteousness."[6] Dyrness writes, "The key to much of modern aesthetics is the autonomy of form and the purity of aesthetic experience. In the Old Testament the contrast that we have seen is not between beauty and ugliness but between beauty in its setting, serving God's purposes, and beauty that is prostituted by leading away from the just order that God intended."[7]

DAUGHTERS OF SARAH

Peter roots his exhortation in the example of "the holy women of the past who put their hope in God" (1 Pet 3:5). By calling these Christian women daughters of Sarah, he gives these women, many of whom were Gentiles, a whole new tradition to draw on. "The Greek moral philosophers are now to be replaced with the writings of Yahweh's prophets. This is another way Peter subtly subverts Greco-Roman culture."[8] Sarah exemplifies submission, even as the relationship between Abraham and Sarah stand as a paradigm of mutual love worked out in a fallen and broken world.

Instead of making women feel inferior, Peter's admonition empowers women. He underscores the difference between the fear of the Lord and the fear of what other people think. He affirms the difference between biblical perfection and cultural perfection. Peter envisions a woman whose confidence and competence exudes her newfound status as a daughter of Sarah. Her sense of awe and reverence for God overcomes her fears of inferiority, intimidation, self-doubt, and timidity. By fearing the Lord she is not fearful of her husband. Through dependence and devotion to God she gains an

---

5. Dyrness, "Aesthetics in the Old Testament," 422.
6. Ibid., 430.
7. Ibid., 431.
8. Jobes, *1 Peter*, 206.

essential perspective for dealing with life. You'll never find her on the cover of *Vogue*, but you will find her in the household of God.

A friend was on a subway in New York City when she observed an overweight, sloppily-dressed woman reading *Cosmopolitan* magazine. This is the kind of magazine that depicts virtual reality women, whose pictures are carefully composed and computer enhanced. It is debatable whether such women exist in real life. The woman's child was at her side clamoring for attention, but she paid him no attention. She treated her son with total indifference as she concentrated on the glossy pictures of models portraying a world far beyond her own. My friend's observation was that this mother was escaping her world and sacrificing her son in the process. The real world was at her knee calling for love, but her mind was filled with false images of perfection.

Peter intends the conduct of Christian women to model authentic discipleship to the entire household of God. The fear of the Lord opposes the fear of what others might think. It shrinks the fears that confine us to the small world of other people's expectations. As we respond to God in reverence and awe, we react less and less to the pressures that intimidate and belittle us.

"YOU HUSBANDS"

Until now Peter has been addressing people who have little or no authority: subjects, slaves, and wives. By contrast, in the Greco-Roman world, husbands in their own households had absolute authority. Nevertheless, believing husbands are instructed along the same lines as slaves and wives. "Husbands, in the same way be considerate . . ." (1 Pet 3:7). Husbands are commanded to "show proper respect for everyone, love the family of believers, fear God, honor the emperor" (1 Pet 2:17). Like slaves, husbands are to live in reverent fear of God (1 Pet 2:18), and like their wives, they are to value inner character over outward social status.

Peter exhorts husbands to be considerate and knowledgeable as they live with their wives. In the light of what Peter has said about being "conscious of God" (1 Pet 2:17) and living "in reverent fear" (1 Pet 1:17; 3:2), to be "knowledgeable" meant that husbands should be "informed by the character of Christ who redeemed you and the overarching purpose of God."[9] Therefore, husbands are to live together with their wives in a way that "is

---

9. Green, *1 Peter*, 100.

Mutual Love

neither demanding nor selfish in his sexual and marital relations; he is instead considerate, sensitive, and serving."[10] They are to show respect to their wives as "the weaker partner" and as coheirs of the gracious gift of life. By coupling a woman's physical weakness to her spiritual status, Peter removes any sense of inferiority.[11] This is a case of compassionate sensitivity, not chauvinistic superiority. A woman's physical weakness relative to a man's strength, however, is not the only weakness in view here. It is clear from the context "that the female is also weaker in the sense of social entitlement and empowerment."[12] Thankfully the situation is changing and women are being accepted equally in all spheres of society.[13] First Peter endorses and encourages mutual submission in Christ.

Husbands are to relate to their wives as well as to other women in the household of faith in three ways: first out of a reverent fear of God; second in sensitivity and respect to sisters in Christ and coheirs of the gracious gift of life; and thirdly in order that God would hear their prayers. Peter's warning was practical, not magical. Disobedience does not produce some kind of hex, but it does indicate a hardness of heart that is offensive to God.[14] The failure to integrate our devotion to God with our most intimate relationships hinders our relationship with the Lord. If our marriage does

---

10. McKnight writes, "The verb *synoikeo* ('living together') was especially used for sexual relations between husband and wife (Deut. 22:13; 24:1; 25:5), and that is no doubt the intended meaning here, though obviously not limited to that." McKnight, *1 Peter*, 186.

11. Harink writes, "That females may often be physically 'weaker' than males cannot be used as an excuse for husbands to dominate or abuse their wives.... It is this common sharing in the *gift* graciously given, not the *possession* of a superior physical strength, that establishes men in right relationship with women. For grace is how the gospel works. Males who do not acknowledge and live in the reality of that grace are still in bondage to 'the desires of the flesh that wage war against the soul' (2:11)." Harink, *1 and 2 Peter*, 88–89.

12. Jobes, *1 Peter*, 209.

13. Elliott writes, "To claim today that women are inferior to men and to insist for this reason on the subordination of women to men would fly in the face of everything we know of human biology and of all of the structural social changes that have insured at least the legal equality of all genders and races. 1 Peter cannot be enlisted to criticize or reject such developments as contrary to the will of God. Rather, what one seeks to discover with relation to First Peter is how the good news that once transformed and enlivened a people of old continues to exert transformative and redemptive power in the present. The letter is a message of evangelical encouragement and exhortation rooted in the death and resurrection of Jesus Christ and expressive of the solidarity that all believers, women and men alike, have with their suffering and exalted Lord." Elliott, *1 Peter*, 598.

14. Green, *1 Peter*, 100.

not reflect Christ's love, how can we expect to honor Christ in our worship and devotion?

The shared work of marriage is a spiritual discipline. Both intimacy and responsibility are heightened and intensified in marriage. By divine design, marriage was created to point beyond itself to our union with God in Christ. These two loves, marital love and divine love, romantic love and redemptive love, are meant to support and illuminate each other. The lesser love, the love between husband and wife, is meant to help us grasp more completely the personal intimacy and earnestness of God's love for us. The greater love, God's sacrificial, saving love, is meant to be the source, strength, and standard for human love. The power and intensity of the oneness experienced between a man and woman points to the greater mystery of our oneness with God in Christ.

SACRIFICIAL LOVE

Barb is married to Dan, a pastor who spent close to a decade spiritually AWOL. Dan was a good friend who loved preaching and served the church faithfully. When we had Sundays off we visited each other's churches. But for reasons I don't altogether understand he took a negative turn. Dan and Barb socialized with a couple in the church and Dan became emotionally attracted to the other man's wife. The feeling was mutual and the two of them began to spend time together. What exactly led to this emotional affair is hard to say: Was it the pressure of the church? Was it a lack of communication between Dan and Barb? Was Dan going through a mid-life crisis? Or was it a combination of all of the above? In any case, there was no good reason for Dan's behavior. Before he separated from Barb and was suspended from his pastoral ministry, Barb and Dan met with my wife and me over lunch to talk it through. I remember when Dan said, "I'd rather spend fifteen minutes with this other woman than three hours with Barb," and seeing Barb literally wince with pain. Dan's blatant disregard for Barb's feelings and his in-your-face disobedience offered little hope for saving the marriage. But Barb made it clear on long walks with my wife, Virginia, that divorce was not an option. She would remain faithful to her marriage vows no matter what.

"Throughout my years as a married Christian woman," Barb writes,

> I easily gave mental assent to Peter's words in 1 Peter 3:1–7. Of course he was addressing Christian wives who were married to

unbelieving husbands. I thought, "This doesn't apply to me." But when my marriage was rapidly disintegrating, these words became true for me in ways that I never dreamed possible. I loved my husband and desired a healthy and vibrant marriage, but I was clueless about what to do when major troubles arose in our relationship. My human instinct was to panic and run. But God didn't let me run away. Instead, he invited me to run to him and take shelter under the Everlasting Arms, where it was safe. Thus began a long chapter in my life of trusting God more deeply than I had ever done before. It was good that I didn't know ahead of time how long this process was going to take or how painful some of the lessons would be. I wanted a quick solution, but God's ways are not our ways. His purpose for me—for us, is sanctification. It was easy to point a finger at my husband and blame him for our mess. But God took a different tactic. The Holy Spirit began taking the logs out of my own eyes and I trusted Christ to work in my husband's life.

Barb is right, Dan wasn't an "unsaved husband." But he was lost just the same and Barb won him over with her patient endurance, her steadfast love, and her commitment to her God-ordained marriage vows. She was not alone in her struggle. The Spirit of God was working the angles and bringing Dan back to himself. Barb quietly embraced Peter's spiritual direction. She bore the pain of unjust suffering because she was conscious of God (1 Pet 2:19). She was willing to "take it" for Christ's sake and to "follow in his steps" (1 Pet 2:21). Her reluctance to claim personal heroics or chronicle Dan's waywardness fits well with the apostle's quiet revolution. Barb fits Peter's bottom-up profile of the mature believer. If you want to know how to live for Christ, look to the slave who has a bad master, look to the wife who has a difficult husband. We don't think that way today, but we should. The apostles who turned the world upside down turned the social ladder upside down too.

8

Christ's Passion Embraced

Finally, all of you, be like-minded, be sympathetic, love one another, be compassionate and humble. Do not repay evil with evil or insult with insult. On the contrary, repay evil with blessing, because to this you were called so that you may inherit a blessing. For, "Whoever would love life and see good days must keep their tongue from evil and their lips from deceitful speech. They must turn from evil and do good; they must seek peace and pursue it. For the eyes of the Lord are on the righteous and his ears are attentive to their prayer, but the face of the Lord is against those who do evil." Who is going to harm you if you are eager to do good? But even it you should suffer for what is right, you are blessed. "Do not fear their threats; do not fear what they fear."

But in your hearts revere Christ as Lord. Always be prepared to give an answer to everyone who asks you to give the reason for the hope that you have. But do this with gentleness and respect, keeping a clear conscience, so that those who speak maliciously against your good behavior in Christ may be ashamed of their slander.

For it is better, if it is God's will, to suffer for doing good than for doing evil. For Christ also suffered once for sins, the righteous for the unrighteous, to bring you to God. He was put to death in the body but made alive in the Spirit. After being made alive, he went and made proclamation to the imprisoned spirits—to those who were disobedient long ago when God waited patiently in the days of Noah while the ark was being built. In it only a few people, eight in all, were saved through the water, and this water symbolizes baptism that now saves you also—not the removal of dirt from the body but

CHRIST'S PASSION EMBRACED

the pledge of clear conscience toward God. It saves you by the resurrection of Jesus Christ, who has gone into heaven and is at God's right hand—with angels, authorities and powers in submission to him. 1 Peter 3:8-22

The apostle Peter's bottom-up profile of costly discipleship is far more radical than we may realize. *Submission* is critical to 1 Peter's Christ for culture strategy. Subjects submit to the emperor. Slaves submit to their masters. Wives submit to their unbelieving husbands. Husbands submit to the needs of their wives. The motivation for this holy submission lies exclusively in the suffering of Christ. "To this you were called, because Christ suffered for you, leaving you an example, that you should follow in his steps" (1 Pet 2:21). Submission uses social hostility as an opportunity *under pressure* to reveal the goodness of God. Sacrifice is the leverage of the gospel.

SURVIVAL SKILLS

The writer Malcolm Gladwell describes an intriguingly similar strategy in his best-selling book *David and Goliath*. His thesis is that underdogs have an uncanny way of overcoming the odds. Israel's shepherd boy conquers the towering Philistine with a small smooth stone. "We spend a lot of time thinking about the ways that prestige and resources and belonging to elite institutions make us better off," says Gladwell. "We don't spend enough time thinking about the ways in which those kinds of material advantages limit our options."[1] Too much of a good thing can be a problem. Too much money makes parenting difficult. Acceptance into an Ivy League school may ruin a good student. Better to be a big fish in a little pond than a little fish in a big pond. "We have, I think, a very rigid and limited definition of what an advantage is," writes Gladwell. "We think of things as helpful that actually aren't and think of other things as unhelpful that in reality leave us stronger and wiser."[2] Dyslexia is a real handicap, not to be wished on anyone, but for some people it inspires great success. Likewise, a horrible childhood may inspire the courage and resilience to become a doctor who fights childhood leukemia with ever fiber of his being.

    Gladwell tells the story of the weak who find the courage to expose the weakness of the powerful and rise above them. He discovers the underdog

---

1. Gladwell, *David and Goliath*, 36.
2. Ibid., 25.

strategies that miraculously beat the odds. "The powerful are not as powerful as they seem—nor the weak as weak."³ Gladwell sees the world differently. Like Peter, he turns the world upside down. He reveals the advantages of disadvantages and the disadvantages of advantages.

But unlike Peter, Gladwell describes the ingenious strategies that help the weak prevail. Backed against the wall, the weak discover a way to trump their powerful foes. David dropped Goliath with a small stone slung with the force of a bullet. Dyslexics become innovators and entrepreneurs because they learn to work outside the system, even if it means bluffing and deceiving to succeed. Gladwell describes the survival tactics of the weak: how they exploit the strength of their opponents to turn it to their advantage. *David and Goliath* is about leveraging your weakness to gain the upper hand. It is about finding a clever way to conquer your opponent.

On the contrary, Peter's resident aliens overcome evil with God's goodness. There are no *devious* or *clever* strategies to change the world. No big plan to outsmart the system. Only the Jesus way and the principle of the cross—my life for yours—instead of the principle of the world—your life for mine. First Peter is not about survival skills or competing as an underdog. It is about being the messianic community marked by the cross. These outposts of hope love life and seek good days.

NO-FEAR SOLIDARITY

Peter used just nine Greek words, including five imperatival adjectives, to describe the household of God. "Finally, all of you: be like-minded, be sympathetic, be loving of brothers and sisters, be tenderhearted, and be humble-minded" (1 Pet 3:8). The order of the words suggest a chiastic structure.⁴ At the center is the kinship love between brothers and sisters in Christ. This familial love shares a common passion for Christ and an abiding love for one another. Instead of translating "sympathetic" along the lines of compassion, Harink stresses the messianic community's "shared passion" for Christ.⁵

To be "tenderhearted" means that believers long for one another with the affection of Christ Jesus (Phil 1:8). Finally, this Christ-centered love is surrounded and defined by a genuine commitment to like-mindedness and

---

3. Ibid., 268.
4. Elliott, *1 Peter*, 603.
5. Harink, *1 and 2 Peter*, 90.

humble-mindedness. Like-mindedness is not a polite consensus celebrating diversity, nor an agreement to get along in spite of serious theological and ethical differences. This is the "shared intelligence" that embraces the truths expounded in 1 Peter.[6] This is the solidarity of the triune-shaped identity, based on the atoning sacrifice of Christ, obedient to the call to holiness, and committed to abstaining from sinful desires. Humble-mindedness is nothing less than cultivating the mind of Christ: "let this mind be in you which was also in Christ Jesus" (Phil 2:5). It is the Beatitude-based mind-set that never graduates from humble service, but always serves the other in the name and manner of Christ himself.[7]

These five imperatives unite the mind and heart, integrate the personal and social, and affirm the priesthood of all believers. Given this description of love and humility in the household of God the burden of spiritual care does not rest on a few individuals. All believers share equal responsibility to live a life worthy of the calling they have received. Everyone who is in the body is gifted to build up the body. Believers bear with one another but all are expected to bear their own responsibility. In a family there are various degrees of maturity but all are expected to be maturing. Responsibilities differ but all are responsible. The family of God is interdependent without fostering dependency. The weak are strengthened without perpetuating weakness. Brothers and sisters are empowered without enabling immaturity.

Love in the household of faith is matched by the willingness to repay insult, abuse, and reviling with blessing. In the midst of an antagonistic and abusive honor-and-shame culture, Peter emphasized "Jesus' non-retaliatory stance."[8] The get-even strategies that fight fire with fire are eliminated. To curse or retaliate are not options for believers who have been called to bless. They lay down the weapons of deception, slander, pride, and hate, in order to pick up the weapons of truth, prayer, compassion, and kindness. Whether or not this strategy works, it is the right strategy. "By repaying evil and abuse with blessing we participate already in God's economy of blessing. That is neither an easy nor a cheap response to those who would

---

6. Ibid., 90.

7. Elliott writes, "In the highly competitive and stratified world of Greco-Roman antiquity, only those of degraded social status were 'humble,' and humility was regarded as a sign of weakness and shame, an inability to defend one's honor. Thus the high value placed on humility by Israelites and Christians is remarkable." Elliott, *1 Peter*, 605.

8. Ibid., 607.

undermine, shame, or attack us. It may cost us much. But it will never cost us more than we have already been given."[9]

The self-control required to bless your accusers and slanderers is evidence of "a supernatural fruit of the Holy Spirit (Gal 5:23)." Karen Jobes continues, "For it is exactly when we are insulted and treated with malicious intent that we are most tempted to respond in kind by gossip, exaggerating the extent of the fault, or with outright slander. Those who are able not simply to clench their teeth and remain silent but to maintain an inner attitude that allows one to pray sincerely for the well-being of one's adversaries, are truly a witness to the life-changing power of a new identity in Christ."[10]

PSALM 34

In the course of his letter, Peter quoted or alluded to Psalm 34 seven times.[11] He used Psalm 34 as Old Testament commentary on the believer's inherited blessing, the hope of the good life. Peter prayed this psalm with resurrection hope (1 Pet 1:3) in anticipation of everlasting life and in appreciation for God's blessings in daily life: "Whoever would love life and see good days . . ." The person who prays this psalm has been given new birth into a living hope and is therefore inspired and empowered not to retaliate against their abusers and slanders with hateful and deceitful speech.

For Peter the eschatological perspective is immediately practical. It governs how Christ's followers respond to negative criticism. Not only must believers refrain from doing evil, "they must seek peace and pursue it" (1 Pet 3:11). Since God has taken the initiative to bring about our reconciliation, we who have been reconciled in Christ can take the initiative and humble

---

9. Harink, *1 and 2 Peter*, 92.

10. Jobes, *1 Peter*, 218.

11. Karen Jobes's comparison is helpful: 1. "Both start with blessing God" (1 Pet 1:3—Ps 34:1); 2. "The result of seeking the Lord was deliverance from all David's sojournings"(1 Pet 1:17—Ps 34:4); 3. "The absence of shame, highly valued in ancient society, is found in both Psalm 34 and 1 Peter" (1 Pet 2:6—Ps 34:5); 4. "The benefits to those who fear the Lord are found in both the psalm and the epistle" (1 Pet 1:17—Ps 34:7); 5. "The responsiveness of God to the suffering of the righteous" is noted in both (1 Pet 2:17—Ps 34:9, 11); 6. "The 'many afflictions' from which the righteous are delivered are mentioned in both" (1 Pet 3:12—Ps 34:17); 7. "The redemption of the servants of the Lord" is found in both (1 Pet 1:6—Ps 34:19; 1 Pet 1:18 and 2:16—Ps 34:22). Ibid., 221–23.

Christ's Passion Embraced

ourselves. We are freed up to pursue peace because "from now on we regard no one from a worldly point of view" (2 Corinthians 5:16). We have not only been reconciled to God in Christ but we have been given the ministry of reconciliation. Peter's emphasis is in full accord with the Apostle Paul's exhortation: "If it is possible, as far as it depends on you, live at peace with everyone," and "Do not be overcome by evil, but overcome evil with good" (Romans 12:18, 21). Because of the grace of Christ it is possible to "Let the peace of Christ rule in [our] hearts, since as members of one body [we] were called to peace. And be thankful" (Colossians 3:15).

Psalm 34 has a special place in my family, because it was my father's chosen psalm in the last months of his life. He prayed this psalm daily, especially these words:

> The righteous cry out, and the Lord hears them; he delivers them from all their troubles. The Lord is close to the brokenhearted and saves those who are crushed in spirit. The righteous person may have many troubles, but the Lord delivers him from them all; he protects all his bones, not one of them will be broken (Psalm 34:17–20).

My father was forty-eight and dying from stomach cancer when he claimed this psalm. He prayed Psalm 34 as much for his family as he did for himself. For him the hardest thing about dying was trusting in the Lord for the future of his wife and two boys. He knew better than anyone that the psalm was not a guarantee for a trouble-free existence; in fact, just the opposite. The righteous are in trouble, praying for deliverance. They cry out. They're brokenhearted. Their spirits are crushed. Life is hard. But in the end there is redemption. At a certain point you stop praying for physical healing and you begin to pray for resurrection.

The psalmist depicts God's total personal engagement in the believer's situation. The Lord's eyes are on the righteous and his ears are attentive to their prayer, but his angry face disapproves of those who do evil. Christ's followers may think that the Lord is distant and unaware, but Peter reminds them that the Lord is fully present and aware of his righteous servants and those who do evil.

SUFFERING

When Silas read out loud the rhetorical question, "Who is going to harm you if you are eager to do good?" (1 Pet 3:13) to the various gatherings of "chosen outsiders," I imagine some of them let out a groan or at least a sigh. Who, indeed? Judging from the repeated references to suffering, Christ's followers were on the receiving end of considerable hostility in the form of abuse, slander, ridicule, accusation, and denigration.[12] There are no indications in the letter of state-sponsored persecutions, legal retribution, imprisonment, or martyrdom, of the kind noted in the book of Revelation. But Peter describes the recipients of his letter as suffering "grief in all kinds of trials" (1 Pet 1:6) and warns them not to "be surprised at the fiery ordeal that has come upon you" (1 Pet 4:12).

The nature of the opposition described and addressed in 1 Peter makes this letter especially relevant for many of today's believers who are socially ostracized and ridiculed. They may not live in hot zones of life-threatening persecution and state-sponsored oppression, but they experience daily pressure to conceal their faith, compromise their ethics, and conform their conduct to the spirit of the times. This is why 1 Peter is especially important for Christians who live and work in cultures that are increasingly antagonistic to the beliefs and behavior of Christ's followers.

Consider a believer's daily experience on a typical university campus. She starts her day in English class where her professor begins class with a quote from Salman Rushdie: "Literature is where I go to explore the highest and lowest places in human society and in the human spirit, where I hope to find not absolute truth but the truth of the tale, of the imagination and of the heart."[13] He lectures the class on the myth of absolute truth and mocks the notion of divine revelation in the Bible. He equates the Bible with the Book of Mormon and the Quran, and argues that the educated mind cannot tolerate dependence on obsolete creeds and truth claims built on thin air.

Her next class is Introduction to Psychology, taught by the faculty advisor for the LGBTQ club on campus. Class begins with a discussion on repressive sexual patterns in society and family. The professor makes it clear that she will not even entertain the notion that marriage between a man and a woman is normative for society. After class our student heads to her dorm, but to her surprise she finds her roommate in bed with a boyfriend, so she heads for Starbucks. Over a latte she reads for class, Tom

---

12. Elliott writes, "Numerous references to verbal abuse paint a consistent picture of the type of opposition and oppression encountered by the Asia Minor believers: suspicion, slander, and insult designed to demean and discredit persons perceived as different, deviant, and potentially dangerous to the common good." Elliott, *1 Peter*, 631.

13. Rushdie, Wikiquote.

Wolfe's latest, *Back to Blood*. If Wolfe is right we are a far more decadent culture than she had ever imagined. He describes a world devoid of friendship and even common decency. His characters are oversexed adult adolescents. Later in the day she meets up with friends and heads to an evening meeting of an on-campus ministry. The speaker's talk is titled "Breathing Room." It is a nice talk with some good jokes and stories about messy roommates and busy schedules, and the need to clean up the clutter in our lives, but it all leaves her feeling empty.

On a typical day Christians on a university campus face a constant verbal and mental assault on their faith and ethics. Believers are subject to a constant flood of perspectives that threaten to overwhelm and undermine their faith. Outright deception, accusation, and slander flow in the same cultural current as innocuous speech about sports, fashion, business, and pop culture. The propaganda stream against the people of God can be both intense and pervasive.

To "suffer for what is right" receives a broad definition in 1 Peter. Suffering is not simply an illness or an accident or a difficult family situation. It is not the hectic pace one may be expected to keep at work or a frustration of personal ambition. It is not increased mortgage rates or an economic downturn. Nor is suffering some inward psychological feeling of empathy with Jesus' suffering. We trivialize suffering if we define it according to an array of everyday calamities that come upon us, irrespective of our commitment to Christ and his kingdom ethic. To "suffer for what is right" (1 Pet 3:17) has a more definite, specifically Christian meaning, which rules out any superficial equating of negative circumstances with the practical reality of taking up our cross and following Jesus.

With that said, we can affirm with Peter that "all kinds of trials" impact believers when they are committed to following Christ. Peter sought to convince believers subject to harsh slave masters that by doing good in their difficult situation they were glorifying God. Likewise, wives of unbelieving husbands who responded to their husbands with the "unfading beauty of a gentle and quiet spirit" (1 Pet 3:4) honored Jesus Christ. It is too narrow to say that Christian suffering is limited to "the political, legally-to-be-expected result of a moral clash with the powers ruling his society."[14]

The world's actions do not define Christian suffering. Suffering for the cause of Christ is determined by how believers respond to negative circumstances. A cancer diagnosis is not necessarily Christian suffering but facing

---

14. Yoder, *The Politics of Jesus*, 129.

cancer for the sake of Christ and with the hope of Christ can turn suffering cancer into genuine cross-bearing. Unemployment is not necessarily Christian suffering but experiencing a difficult and possibly humiliating situation with the humility and hope of Christ transforms a negative circumstance into positive Christian witness.

To "suffer for what is right" may specifically mean for you rejection by other professing believers because you have seemingly taken Jesus and his teaching too seriously and passionately. It may result in scorn and ridicule from those who deny God's clear commands regarding sexuality and the maintenance of physical and psychological health. Taking up your cross may result in a job demotion because you are not willing to sacrifice your life and family for the sake of the company. It may result in dismissal because you will not permit a specific injustice to go unnoticed.

Christian suffering will mean the real sacrifice of our material possessions for the sake of the body of Christ. Taking up our cross may mean the costly inconvenience of practicing law in the inner city among the poor or medicine in the war-ravaged Congo for the sake of the gospel. For many of our cross-cultural missionaries and developing world brothers and sisters, taking up Jesus' cross may lead to being falsely accused regarding political motives because of their opposition to social and political injustices. Christian suffering may mean courageously facing the reality of a mentally disabled son or daughter in the spirit of love and confidence that Jesus Christ both wills and provides.

It should also be said that many who think they are suffering for Christ's sake are suffering for themselves, not for Christ. They are not filled with Christ's love and humility, they are filled with fear and anger and resentment. They are ready to meet insult with insult and slander with slander. The people of God were meant to be like Joseph in Pharaoh's Egypt and Daniel in Nebuchadnezzar's Babylon. We are salt and light in a fallen world. If the household of God follows the example of Jesus, the world has nothing to fear from Christians and everything to gain, but, like Jesus, his followers will be marked by the cross.

SALVATION'S HOPE

We come to one of the most familiar passages in 1 Peter, but we come from a different angle. Instead of using this text as a motivation for amassing intellectual arguments in defense of the faith, Peter challenges believers to sanctify Christ as Lord in their hearts. Instead of playing on the fears of naive believers who feel threatened and frightened by the culture wars, Peter calls believers to revere Christ as Lord. Uppermost in his mind is the prophet Isaiah's warning: "Do not call conspiracy everything this people calls a conspiracy; do not fear, and do not dread it. The Lord Almighty is the one you are to regard as holy, he is the one you are to fear, he is the one you are to dread" (Isa 8:12–13).

Conspiracy theories abound in popular Christianity, promoted by fearmongers who would like nothing better than to work up Christians into a frenzy of concern. Peter warns against falling for these fear tactics and challenges believers to cultivate fear of the Lord. Forget the culture wars and the campaigns to take back America. Stop with the hand-wringing over gay marriage, legalized marijuana, and abortion. Yes, these are serious issues that call for unity in truth and practice among confessing believers, but in terms of relating to the culture they are side issues. Peter is not calling for Christians to make their best case against evolutionary materialism, gay marriage, and smoking pot. He is calling Christians to live so radically under the lordship of Jesus Christ that people are bound to ask the reason for their hope in Christ.

"Hope" for Peter was like "faith" for Paul. In a single word it sums up the people of God's shared belief in the gospel of Jesus Christ. This is the hope that drives out fear because we have been given new birth into a living hope. Our identity in God the Father, Son, and Holy Spirit cannot be stolen. Our eternal salvation, experienced now and in the future, cannot be taken from us. Our destiny cannot be diverted. This is the hope that "does not close doors to relationship with other people out of either fear or hate. It turns, rather, in openness to others just as it turns to God."[15]

The sanctifying process of setting apart Christ as Lord in our hearts is evident in how well we relate to a hostile world. Effectiveness is measured not in eloquence or brilliance, much less in manipulation or coercion, but in gentleness, respect, and a clear conscience. Peter's apology (ἀπολογίαν) is rooted in a believer's transformed life and delivered with the utmost courtesy.[16] The medium of gospel communication is gentleness, respect, and

---

15. Goppelt, *A Commentary on 1 Peter*, 243.

16. Harink writes, "The Christian theological discipline of apologetics is often tempted to locate the social, cultural, and intellectual strongholds of a given society and then argue from them to the gospel, or assimilate the gospel to them, or render the gospel in their terms, in order to show that the Christian faith is aligned with and supported by, rather than alien to, such strongholds. But that strategy usually amounts

good behavior. Ordinary people with whom we work and play are asking for an explanation "concerning the hope that is in you" (1 Pet 3:15). This is the hope that sets believers apart and arouses their neighbors' curiosity and even their antagonism and slander.[17] Karl Barth commented on how Christians ought to speak to non-Christians:

> We must not sit among them like melancholy owls, but in a certainty about our goal, which surpasses all other certainty. Yet how often we stand ashamed beside the children of the world, and how we must understand them if our message will not satisfy them. He who knows that "my times are in your hands" (Ps 31:15) will not haughtily regard the [people] of the world, who, in a definite hope that often shames us, go their way; but he will understand them better than they understand themselves. He will see their hope as a parable, a sign that the world is not abandoned, but has a beginning and a goal. We Christians have to put the right Alpha and Omega into the heart of this secular thought and hope. But we can only do so if we surpass the world in confidence.[18]

The true spirit of Peter's apologetic message is captured in Cormac McCarthy's drama *The Sunset Limited*. The one-act play is a conversation between a black man and white man (referred to simply as Black and White) that takes place in a New York City ghetto. In the movie version, Samuel L. Jackson brings the white professor, played by Tommy Lee Jones, back to his apartment after rescuing him from a suicide attempt. Black tries to convince White that life is worth living, because he wants assurance that White won't throw himself in front of a train again. The ensuing conversation is a brilliant back-and-forth point-counterpoint between an ex-con who has found real hope in Christ and a professor who has given up on life. Black's simple faith is in dialogue with White's sophisticated nihilism. In the end, White says,

> I'm sorry. You're a kind man, but I have to go. I've heard you out and you've heard me and there's no more to say. Your God must have once stood in a dawn of infinite possibility and this is what he's made of it. And now it is drawing to a close. You say that I want God's love. I don't. Perhaps I want forgiveness, but there is no one to ask it of. And there is no going back. No setting things right.

to the cancellation of the gospel rather than the defeat of the strongholds." Harink, *1 and 2 Peter*, 94.

17. Elliott, *1 Peter*, 628.
18. Barth, *Dogmatics in Outline*, 132.

Christ's Passion Embraced

> Perhaps once. Not now. Now there is only the hope of nothingness. I cling to that hope. Now open the door. Please.[19]

Black reluctantly undoes the bolts, opens the door, and the professor exits. Black collapses to his knees, all but weeping. He feels utterly defeated in his attempt to rescue White and convince him of the hope he has in Christ. In desperation, he looks up, and cries out to God, "He didn't mean them words. You know he didn't."

And then he says something that corresponds to Peter's exhortation "to always be prepared to give an answer . . . for the hope you have." Black says, "I don't understand what you sent me down there for. I don't understand it. If you wanted me to help him how come you didn't give me the words? You give em to him. What about me?" Black kneels, weeping. Then, he says, "That's all right. That's all right. If you never speak again you know I'll keep your word. You know I will. You know I'm good for it." He lifts his head. "Is that okay? Is that okay?"

Black's sense of inadequacy and apparent inability to meet the professor's intellectual arguments are feelings commonly shared by Christians who seek to give an answer for the hope they have. We feel Black's deep sense of defeat, even despair, at our inability to convince the world of our hope in Christ. We ask along with him, why doesn't God give us just the right words to knock down the nihilist's arguments or the hedonist's philosophy or the religionist's system? But Peter wasn't looking for a bulletproof apologetic. On the contrary, he called believers to live humbly, boldly, without fear. He encouraged them to set apart Christ as Lord in their innermost being. He challenged them to obey the Word, not have all the right words. Black acquired this insight painfully, but expressed it beautifully, when he said to God, "If you never speak again you know I'll keep your word."[20]

CHRIST'S PASSION AND OURS

Peter's Christ for culture strategy is grounded in the atoning sacrifice of Christ. The reason it is better "to suffer for doing good than for doing evil" is because of Christ's triumph on the cross. The answer or apology (ἀπολογίαν) that Christ's followers give "to everyone who asks you to give the reason for the hope you have" is the story of the cross. Christ's passion

---

19. McCarthy, *The Sunset Limited*, 141.
20. Ibid., 142.

is foundational to everything the people of God have to say to the world. We are called to enter into Christ's passion narrative, not as little messiahs trying to save the world, but as humble disciples following our Master. What the world needs most is the gospel of Jesus Christ. Wherever possible the people of God advocate for social justice, humanitarian benefits, and political reform, but two realities must always be kept in mind. First, only Christ can bring about the justice and shalom the human heart longs for. No amount of contribution to and cooperation with the world will achieve God's will apart from the cross. Second, the complexity and depravity of the human condition means that unintended negative consequences inevitably trail behind the pursuit of social and political justice and humanitarian effort.

The reason Christians can submit graciously to harsh bosses and unbelieving spouses is because Christ suffered for us: "once for sins, the righteous for the unrighteous, to bring [us] to God" (1 Pet 3:18). The reason we can repay evil with blessing is because of Christ's crucifixion, resurrection, and ascension. The incarnational strategy of submission works because Christ has triumphed over sin and death. Christ "is at God's right hand—with angels, authorities and powers in submission to him" (1 Pet 3:22).

Considerable research and speculation has been invested in Peter's intriguing statement: "After being made alive, he went and made proclamation to the imprisoned spirits—to those who were disobedient long ago when God waited patiently in the days of Noah while the ark was being built" (1 Pet 3:19–20). Simply stated, 1 Peter anchors the rationale for the cruciform life in salvation history. Peter reaches all the way back to Genesis 6 and describes two groups of people. The first group are "imprisoned spirits" who were "disobedient" in the days of Noah. The second group includes Noah and seven others who trusted in God and were saved from the flood. From the beginning of time, Christ's death and resurrection have been pivotal for human history. God's mercy has always been rooted in the atoning sacrifice of Christ. This is the good news proclaimed by the risen Christ to all humanity and to the cosmic powers for time and eternity.[21]

---

21. Christ's proclamation takes place after the resurrection. It is a declaration to all creatures across all times of the victory of the cross. Tradition credits 1 Peter 3:19 as the source for the phrase in the Apostles' Creed that says Jesus "descended into hell." Instead of speculating on an intermediate state between Jesus' death and resurrection, it is better to keep the plain sense of the text. After Jesus died and rose again he proclaimed the gospel to the living and the dead through the Spirit of Christ. Harink suggests that the Apostles' Creed might better read, "He was crucified, died, and was buried. He entered

Christ's Passion Embraced

Peter compares the culture of disobedience, which is great in number, to the faithful presence of the much smaller messianic community of baptized believers. Noah and seven others are saved from the flood. Their faithfulness in the midst of dominating disobedience is an inspiration and model for believers everywhere. The physical act of baptism does not save, but when it is received by faith as a sign of Christ's atoning sacrifice and bodily resurrection, it is the "pledge of a clear conscience toward God" (1 Pet 3:21). Although God's chosen outsiders may feel vastly outnumbered, they are honoring God by their faithfulness. The author of Hebrews echoes Peter's application to the people of God: "By faith Noah, when warned about things not seen, in holy fear built an ark to save his family. By his faith he condemned the world and became heir of the righteousness that is in keeping with faith" (Heb 11:7).

Peter's emphasis on the triumph and victory of Christ may seem unusual until we realize how well it resonates with other New Testament texts. The Apostle Paul said, "the mystery from which true godliness springs is great: He appeared in the flesh, was vindicated by the Spirit, was seen by angels, was preached among the nations, was believed on in the world, was taken up in glory" (1 Tim 3:16). To the Colossians, Paul wrote that believers were buried with Christ in baptism. All the charges against them were nailed to the cross and when Christ "disarmed the powers and authorities, he made a public spectacle of them, triumphing over them by the cross" (Col 2:12–15). Peter's *Christus Victor* theme also resonates with the Apostle John's description of salvation history in Revelation 12. There the believers are confronted by Satan, "who leads the whole world astray," but they triumph over him "by the blood of the Lamb and by the word of their testimony; they did not love their lives so much as to shrink from death" (Rev 12:9–11).

If the angels and authorities submit to the risen and ascended Christ, we who have been forgiven, redeemed, and baptized ought to willingly submit to Christ's cruciform pattern of gospel proclamation. We remember Peter's struggle with Jesus' path to the cross, how he resisted Jesus' clear teaching: "that he must be killed and on the third day be raised to life" (Matthew 16:21). Like Peter, we struggle with Christ's theology of submission and sacrifice. We want a path to success, not a path to the cross. But if Peter could change, as he surely did, there is hope for you and me.

---

fully into the reality of death. On the third day he rose again from the dead." Harink, *1 and 2 Peter*, 99.

9

Living God's Way

Therefore, since Christ suffered in his body, arm yourselves also with the same attitude, because whoever suffers in the body is done with sin. As a result, they do not live the rest of their earthly lives for evil human desires, but rather for the will of God.

For you spent enough time in the past doing what pagans choose to do—living in debauchery, lust, drunkenness, orgies, carousing, and detestable idolatry. They are surprised that you do not join them in their reckless, wild living, and they heap abuse on you. But they will have to give account to him who is ready to judge the living and the dead.

For this is the reason the gospel was preached even to those who are now dead, so that they might be judged according to human standards in regard to the body, but live according to God in regard the spirit.

The end of all things is near. Therefore be alert and of sober mind so that you may pray. Above all, love each other deeply, because love covers over a multitude of sins. Offer hospitality to one another without grumbling. Each of you should use whatever gift you have received to serve others, as faithful stewards of God's grace in its various forms. If anyone speaks, they should do so as one who speaks the very words of God. If anyone serves, they should do so with the strength God provides, so that in all things God may be praised through Jesus Christ. To him be the glory and the power for ever and ever. Amen. 1 Peter 4:1–11

Peter brings the cosmic triumph of Christ's atoning sacrifice into the everyday experience of the ordinary believer. He moves from ancient salvation history to practical Christian living. The new paradigm for *living* life is *Christ's suffering*: "Since Christ suffered in his body, arm yourselves also with the same attitude, because whoever suffers in his body is done with sin" (1 Pet 4:1). This is not suffering for suffering's sake; nor suffering for doing wrong. This is gospel-induced suffering because of a believer's faithfulness to the will of God.

JESUS-STYLE MILITANCY

The Roman military presence was pervasive throughout Asia Minor, which may account for Peter's use of military language.[1] Earlier he referred to sinful desires which wage war against the soul (1 Pet 2:11); now he urges believers to arm themselves with the same mind-set as Christ (1 Pet 4:1). Paul used similar language when he challenged believers to put on the full armor of God ("jocking up," as the Navy SEALs say). The apostolic commitment to combat readiness is intentional, but instead of being armed with the "weapons of the world" (2 Cor 10:4), Peter calls for acquiring a Christlike mind-set that is willing to suffer for the good. Karl Barth describes the believer's militancy: "The militant revolt demanded of Christians—and this distinguishes it from all kinds of other revolts—is not directed against people: not even against the host of unbelievers, false believers, and the superstitious . . . nor even . . . against the wicked. . . . In terms of their commission—even though they will sometimes clash with all kinds of people in discharging it—they rebel and fight *for* all men, even, and in the last resort precisely, for those with whom they may clash."[2]

The power of the cross is greater than any military weapon. Peter extols its virtues: "whoever suffers in the body is done with sin" (1 Pet 4:1). The believer's intentional decision to act according to God's will, even though it means suffering the world's hostility, underscores a marked behavioral change. We choose to enter through the narrow gate, because the broad way leads to disobedience and destruction (Matt 7:13–14). We make it our decision "to look after orphans and widows in their distress and to keep [ourselves] from being polluted by the world" (Jas 1:27). We no longer love the world or "anything in the world," because "everything in the world—the

---

1. Elliott, *1 Peter*, 713.
2. Barth, quoted in Harink, *1 and 2 Peter*, 127.

lust of the flesh, the lust of the eyes, and the pride of life—comes not from the Father but from the world" (1 John 2:15–16).

Suffering serves as a discipline, strengthening the believer's moral and ethical actions. We become like Jesus learning obedience by what we suffer (Heb 5:8). We face a choice. We either take "the path of least resistance — going along with the values, norms, and practices" acceptable to society —or we obey the will of God and suffer "the consequences of criticism and condemnation by unbelieving family and friends."[3]

DEFINING ISSUES

The believers in northern Ghana are first-generation Christians. Whenever I am there, I feel like I have stepped back in time to the early church. I feel like I am inside the New Testament, free from the burden of Christendom—Christless Christianity. Nevertheless, syncretistic Christianity is a formidable foe in Ghana as well as in West, because it assimilates popular culture and the spirit of the times into either an ancient animistic past or an ever-changing, progressive, human-made religion. My fellowship with Ghanaian believers who have been converted from animism and spiritism gives me hope for representing Christ to younger generations in the West who are animated by the gods of selfism and materialism.

The stark contrast between paganism and the people of God is not a development to be feared but to be embraced by believers who are willing to suffer for their faith. These Ghanaian believers come out of villages steeped in witchcraft and shamanism. The dangers of idolatry are very real. Villagers sacrifice chickens and goats before wooden idols and sacred stones. Their congregations wrestle with the occult and demonic taboos. As believers break away from these customs they are often blamed for disease and drought and whatever bad thing that happens in the villages. They are shunned and ridiculed. Their livelihood is threatened. Simple acts of faithfulness are costly. Even Christian chiefs are under pressure to prove their loyalty by complying with ancient taboos. These believers, like the first recipients of 1 Peter, know what it is like to suffer for doing what is right.

Peter leverages the pagan lifestyle against new life in Christ. "For you have spent enough time in the past doing what pagans choose to do . . ." (1 Pet 4:3). The contrast between pagan choices and Christian living was easy to see and costly to experience in first-century Asia Minor. In America, and

3. Jobes, *1 Peter*, 265.

especially in the Christian South, where I live, it is more difficult to see the contrast between paganism and Christianity. The line clearly drawn in the first century is blurred in the twenty-first century.

Believers in the West struggle to discern the difference between the will of God and "what pagans choose to do." We are not sure what qualifies as "living in debauchery" and engaging in "detestable idolatry" (1 Pet 4:3). Like the proverbial frog in the kettle we have acclimated to moral degeneracy. "Progressive" Christians claim prohibiting premarital sex, abortion, and homosexual practice is regressive. Sexual freedom and acceptance in the name of love is embraced and celebrated. This softening and sentimentalizing of moral conviction erodes biblical conviction and undermines sexual purity and fidelity. In a generation we have gone from debating the biblical standard on human sexuality to wholesale capitulation in some religious circles to the spirit of the times.

In the interest of full disclosure it becomes an evangelistic imperative to explain why sexual purity outside of marriage and sexual fidelity between a man and a woman in marriage is God's standard for human flourishing. To present the gospel without this teaching only causes confusion down the road. This may make evangelism more challenging, because we don't want pagan notions of sexual freedom to get in the way of a person's freedom to come to Christ. However, we want people to know that coming to Christ involves embracing a biblical sexual ethic. Everyone has sexual sins to repent of—no one is sin-free when it comes to sex—but in Christ we experience the power of guilt-freeing, life-healing forgiveness and the strength to remain faithful. Every generation seems to face a particular challenge to God's will on sex. In my college years it was premarital sex and abortion. Today, the popular issue is homosexual practice and gay marriage. James Houston and Bruce Waltke have observed, "We are old enough to remember a Western world when homosexuality was a vice so frightful in demeanor as to be hated on sight. But then the West pitied that behavior; then treated it as a sickness, and finally the president led the United States to embrace it as a viable lifestyle. The Western nations are becoming hardened in sin and are being cut off from the olive tree of blessing."[4]

Christians who are sensitive to the moral degeneracy of popular entertainment are accused of being puritanical. Over time we have been seduced into thinking that explicit, vulgar sexuality is entertaining and that anything labeled love, no matter how immoral, is acceptable. The seduction

---

4. Houston and Waltke, *The Psalms as Christian Worship*, 135.

of the soul extends far beyond sexual issues to something as seemingly innocuous as a humorous TED Talk. Christians are easily swayed by selective truth packaged in humor. I first heard of behavioral scientist Brené Brown through an evangelical pastor who sang her praises and encouraged his congregation to learn from her the secret of happiness.

Brené Brown claims vulnerability is the key to human relationships. She contends that the secret behind our broken relationships is our failure to confront shame head-on. We are paralyzed by our feelings of insecurity and unworthiness. On the computer screen she displays an ugly swamp and says, "Shame is the swampland of the soul."[5] She encourages us to rise up out of the muck of our feelings of inadequacy and embrace our vulnerability courageously. Brené Brown cuts out all the tough stuff to believe in and boils it all down to vulnerability. She sweeps away the problem of guilt, the depth of depravity, and the need for repentance. Life's solution is found apart from redemption—apart from the atoning sacrifice of Christ. The lie is convenient, practical, and can be told with plenty of humor and fun stories about vulnerability.

The line between paganism and the Christian life is obscured by the subtlety of our modern idolatries. Christians do not bow down to wooden statutes or special rocks, as my Ghanaian brothers did in their former lives, but Western believers are tempted to bow before the gods of sports or success or technology.

Shirl Hoffman, in *Good Game: Christianity and the Culture of Sports*, challenges Christians "to think critically about sports" and "to explore seriously how the sporting culture intersects" with the Christian life.[6] Unwittingly we are drawn into an idolatry that is antithetical to following Christ. Hoffman contends that professional sports are "a grotesque distortion of sports," a cultural obsession that is "narcissistic, materialistic, self-interested, violent, sensational, coarse, racist, sexist, brazen, raunchy, hedonistic, body-destroying, militaristic." Sports "is light years removed from what Christians for centuries have idealized as the embodiment of the gospel message. How Christians, and especially evangelicals, have managed to live in these two diametrically opposed worlds, even to the point of harnessing one to serve the other" is the focus of his concern.[7] As Hoffman says, "We

---

5. Brown, "The Power of Vulnerability."
6. Hoffman, *The Good Game*, xiii.
7. Ibid., 11.

don't go to sporting events to see the Sermon on the Mount in action."[8] Cheating, doping, violence, self-indulgence, and body worship characterize this competitive and enticing religion.

Technology is another cultural idol that threatens Christians. Steve Jobs is an iconic figure in the pantheon of today's techno-Tower of Babel. On Google's maps the plain of Shinar borders Silicon Valley. The people of Shinar sought to preserve human solidarity through technology. In keeping with modern aspirations technology is the new salvation. The Lord's assessment of their efforts underscores the danger of human solidarity when it is not in union with God. The Lord said, "If as one people speaking the same language they have begun to do this, then nothing they plan to do will be impossible for them" (Gen 11:6). The triune God thwarted the Shinar project by confusing their language, rendering them unable to understand one another. The Tower of Babel and its quest for salvation through technology is a religious ideology that is still in play today.

Steve Jobs believed that innovative products go beyond meeting physical needs and serve to satisfy deep spiritual needs. Jobs married Eastern spirituality with Western materialism. The "I" in iPod, iPhone, iTunes, iPad, and iCloud stands for Apple's resolve to create devices seamlessly integrated with the Internet.[9] But you could be forgiven if you thought that the iconic "I" represents the autonomous self. Seamless connectivity between the Internet and a device has become more than a tool. Technology morphs into a philosophy of life that preaches solidarity (salvation) in the cyber-world. The mesmerizing myth of wholeness through sexy devices substitutes for intimate community.

Steve Jobs offered the iconic apple as the forbidden fruit, flipping the biblical message of the fall of man. In this post-Christian myth it is God who lies and the devil who speaks truth when the serpent says, "For God knows that when you eat of it your eyes will be opened, and you will be like God, knowing good and evil" (Gen 3:5). Andy Crouch writes, "That bitten apple was just one of Steve Jobs's many touches of genius, capturing the promise of technology in a single glance." He "turned Eve's apple, the symbol of fallen humankind, into a religious icon for true believers in technology." Jobs was able to "to articulate a perfectly secular form of hope." He was "the perfect evangelist because he had no competing source of hope." "This is the gospel of a secular age," explains Crouch. "It has the great virtue

8. Ibid., 156.
9. Isaacson, *Steve Jobs*, 338.

of being based only on what we can all perceive—it requires neither revelation nor dogma. And it promises nothing it cannot deliver—since all that is promised is the opportunity to live your own unique life, a hope that is manifestly realizable since it is offered by one who has so spectacularly succeeded by following his own 'inner voice, heart and intuition.'"[10]

The modern pantheon of gods and goddesses rivals that of the ancient Greek pantheon. Peter refers to "detestable idolatry" (1 Pet 4:3), implying that the choice between right and wrong, good and evil, was clear and straightforward. But the danger of modern idolatry is that it is subtle, soft, and deceptively safe. Believers in Asia Minor stopped going to the theater but we can watch lewd performances in our living rooms. The brutality, violence, and inhumanity of the gladiatorial fights kept Christians away from the games, but we pay 1,500 dollars for Super Bowl tickets. They refused to burn incense to the emperor, but we pay homage to the imperial self. The reason we do not suffer the abuse and slander that the early Christians did may be because the world sees no difference between themselves and Christians.[11]

First Peter's original recipients crossed a chasm from their old pagan lifestyle to a radically new life in Christ. Once they were not a people, but now they were the people of God (1 Pet 2:10). Formerly, they lived in debauchery, lust, drunkenness, orgies, carousing, and detestable idolatry; now they declared the praises of him who called them out of darkness into his wonderful light (1 Pet 2:9). Their conversion did not meet with the world's approval.

UNIVERSAL JUDGMENT

Pagans, ancient and modern, like the notion that "What happens in Vegas stays in Vegas." They identify with the old tag line, "You only go around once in life so you've got to grab for all the gusto you can." The idea persists that death ends all. Charles Bukowski's poem "The Laughing Heart" captures the ethos of the age: "your life is your life, don't let it be clubbed into dank submission. . . . you can't beat death but you can beat death in

---

10. Crouch, "Steve Jobs."

11. McKnight writes, "In the present passage, the main thrust is the moral value of suffering, a thrust that is largely outside the normal experience of the vast majority of Western Christians today." McKnight, *1 Peter*, 229.

life."[12] Pagans who heap abuse on Christ's followers because they "do not join them in their reckless, wild living" will have "to give an account to him who is ready to judge the living and the dead" (1 Pet 4:4–5).

The Bible says a great deal about the judgment of God, much more than many Christians care to admit. Salvation history is replete with warning, admonition, correction and condemnation. Humankind is "put on notice." Warning gives way to verdict and indictment leads to sentencing. Catastrophic judgment is described from beginning to end. God is deadly serious about finishing off evil once and for all.

The reality of divine judgment is an important reason for preaching the gospel to "the living and the dead" (1 Pet 4:5). Humanity—past, present, and future—is destined for God's judgment. Peter used this same phrase with Cornelius, when he said, "He commanded us to preach to the people and to testify that he is the one whom God appointed as judge of the living and the dead" (Acts 10:42; see also 2 Tim 4:1). Peter is not implying that those who had died have a second opportunity to hear the gospel.[13] What he is saying is that the gospel preached to the living and "even to those now dead" (1 Pet 4:6) declares their accountability to God. Those who have been persecuted and oppressed by people who refused to respond to the good news of Jesus Christ will be held accountable.

THE NEW NORMAL

Peter concludes this section with a brief exhortation followed by a benediction. In rapid succession he delivers a series of imperatives. Christian virtues are set in contrast to pagan vices (1 Pet 4:3). Two radically different lifestyles are placed in bold relief to accentuate their divergent world views. While the world continues to push a way of living that is physically, emotionally, and spiritually destructive, the household of faith exists to love and serve others and honor and glorify God.

"The end of all things is near" (1 Pet 4:7). The pagan belief that there is no universal judgment and death ends all is contrasted with the conviction

---

12. Bukowski, "The Laughing Heart," 400.

13. Elliott writes, "The notion of a second opportunity for repentance and life offered to those who died before Christ is thoroughly inconsistent with the theology, ethics, and aim of 1 Peter as a whole. In this letter the stress consistently falls on the performance of the will of God here and now, and judgment according to one's behavior in the present." Elliott, *1 Peter*, 731.

that the end of the ages is in the hands of the just and holy God. Christ's followers believe that the true goal or end of history has been reached in the death and resurrection of Jesus Christ. Hope is based on "the coming salvation that is ready to be revealed in the last time" (1 Pet 1:5, 20). Peter sets a contrast between the pagan perception of a nihilistic never-ending circle of life and the believer's hope of salvation and the culmination of God's rule and reign.

"Therefore be alert and of sober mind so that you may pray" (1 Pet 4:7). Believers are encouraged to be self-controlled, clear minded, and vigilant. The hallmark of Peter's spiritual direction is its practical, down-to-earth, daily character. The confusion and emotional turmoil of "debauchery, lust, drunkenness, orgies, carousing and detestable idolatry" (1 Pet 4:3) gives way to sober thinking, caring love, and prayer.

"Above all, love each other deeply, because love covers a multitude of sins" (1 Pet 4:8). Peter makes love "the core and chief characteristic of the community."[14] Instead of a "love" that uses people to feed one's lustful appetites and sensual pleasures, this love (ἀγάπην) refuses to use people up. This love "covers over a multitude of sins" (1 Pet 4:8). It neither atones for sin, because only God can atone for sins, nor does it ignore or deny or cover up sin.[15] This love "unflinchingly acknowledges the sins of others and yet, absorbing the cost, 'covers' those sins over and over again with grace and forgiveness . . . ."[16] Peter may have in mind the proverb that says, "Hatred stirs up conflict, but love covers over all wrongs" (Prov 10:12).

Kierkegaard reasoned in *Works of Love* that our duty is not to find "the lovable object" but to find the person before us lovable. Actual love, loving the person before us, is always concrete and often sacrificial. "Truth takes a firm step," says Kierkegaard, "and for that reason sometimes a difficult one, too." The opposite of actual love is a theory of love focused on the ideal. "Delusion is always floating; for that reason it sometimes appears quite light and spiritual, because it is so airy."[17] We are to love our children, coworkers, neighbors, and strangers, not because we have chosen to love them, but because Christ calls us to love them.

My hunch is that none of us need to look very far to find a challenging person to love. A day after rereading Kierkegaard on love, I received

---

14. Harink, *1 and 2 Peter*, 113.
15. Jobes, *1 Peter*, 279.
16. Harink, *1 and 2 Peter*, 113.
17. Kierkegaard, *Works of Love*, 158–61.

an accusatory email from a church member. His criticism against me and others felt deep-seated and meanspirited. My immediate impulse was to fire back an angry email to set the record straight and to defend myself. But Kierkegaard's intrusive reminder to love as Christ loved was stuck in my mind. I remember wishing it wasn't. We never have far to look for a person to love who is impossible to love apart from the grace of God. Actual love is for the real people with whom we must deal with daily. Airy love is a fine sounding theory filled with ethereal possibilities.

The world's idea of love, says Kierkegaard, is "group-selfishness." The world rightly condemns me-only self-love as selfish, but when selfishness forms a group of other selfish people the world calls it love. The world demands that selfish people give up a measure of selfishness in order to enjoy the privileges of group-selfishness. This kind of love sacrifices the God-relationship and "locks God out or at most takes him along for the sake of appearance."[18] Sanctioned self-love comes in many forms: ethnic compatibility, tribal affinity, denominational loyalty, social familiarity, and generational identity. But to love as Christ loves is to know the difference between "group-selfishness" and being the neighbor Christ calls us to be.

"Offer hospitality to one another without grumbling" (1 Pet 4:9). Christians are homeless outsiders who have found their true home in the household of God. Although they have been marginalized, ostracized, slandered, mocked, accused, and denigrated by mainstream culture, they are commanded to befriend the stranger. When we open our homes to friends and strangers, set the table, put on a meal, and break bread together, we invite God's blessing. This pattern of hospitality is at the heart of the gospel. Food for the body and food for the soul belong together. Spirituality is often squeezed into a corner of life reserved for pious reflections and church services. But God intended spirituality to be at the center of our ordinary, everyday life together.

The Holy Spirit has assured us that there is a deep-level mystery involved in hospitality. We meet Christ in the midst of relating to others. "Inasmuch as you have done it to the least of these, you have done it unto me" (Matt 25:40). "Do not forget to show hospitality to strangers, for by so doing some people have shown hospitality to angels without knowing it" (Heb 13:2).

Hospitality has greater rewards than most of us imagine: "Anyone who welcomes you welcomes me, and anyone who welcomes me welcomes the

---

18. Ibid., 123.

one who sent me" (Matt 10:40). The measure of our openness to others reveals our intimacy with the one who said, "Come unto me" (Matt 11:28). One of the best-kept secrets about hospitality is that those who offer it benefit more than those who receive it. We think of hospitality as giving to others, but what if hospitality is the Lord's way of bringing people into our lives who will give to us: the foreign student who enlargers our world, the homeless person who deepens our compassion, the missionary who causes us to pray more earnestly, the single mom who increases our family, and the neighbor whose presence next door trains us in practical love? We may be like the reluctant widow at Zarephath, entertaining the prophet Elijah, or like the eager-hearted Lydia hosting the Apostle Paul. Hospitality was meant to be an opportunity, not an imposition.

"Each of you should use whatever gift you have received to serve others, as faithful stewards of God's grace in its various forms. If anyone speaks, they should do so as one who speaks the very words of God. If anyone serves, they should do so with the strength God provides, so that in all things God may be praised through Jesus Christ." The generosity of the household of God is in marked contrast to the competitive self-serving nature of the pagan culture. There is no reason to think that Peter is focused primarily on material resources or that he excluded any of the gifts the Apostle Paul identified (Rom 12:6–8; 1 Cor 12:8–10; Eph 4:11). Peter implied the full range of gifts when he spoke of "God's grace in its various forms" and "whatever gift you have received" (1 Pet 4:10). Every living stone has something to contribute to the building up of the household of God. Everyone bears with one another and everyone is expected to bear his or her own responsibility. Responsibilities differ but all are responsible. We are interdependent without fostering dependency. We strengthen the weak without perpetuating weakness. We empower one another without enabling immaturity.

"If anyone speaks" and "If anyone serves" (1 Pet 4:11) imply the fullness of the gifts, because "speaking" and "serving" bracket the full range of ministry.[19] To speak is to speak the very words of God. To serve is to do so with the strength God provides. All spiritual gifts are dependent on God's will and power. There are no spiritual gifts, no works of service, designed to build up the body that can work effectively apart from the wisdom and guidance of the word of God. The ministry of the word is essential in the use of all the spiritual gifts.

---

19. Jobes, *1 Peter*, 281.

Living God's Way

God's chosen outsiders distinguish themselves by their grasp of reality and their salvation hope. They are alert, sober-minded, and prayerful. They love one another deeply. They forgive easily. They cut each other slack. They are eager to offer hospitality and use God's gifts for his kingdom purposes. In their speech and service they are God-dependent. They are submissive to the Lord Jesus Christ in all things. He alone is their mediator and model for how to bring glory to God. "To him be the glory and the power for ever and ever. Amen" (1 Pet 4:11).

10

A Christ for Culture Strategy

Dear friends, do not be surprised at the fiery ordeal that has come on you to test you, as though something strange were happening to you. But rejoice inasmuch as you participate in the sufferings of Christ, so that you may be overjoyed when his glory is revealed.

If you are insulted because of the name of Christ, you are blessed, for the Spirit of glory and of God rests on you. If you suffer, it should not be as a murderer or thief or any other kind of criminal, or even as a meddler. However, if you suffer as a Christian, do not be ashamed, but praise God that you bear that name.

For it is time for judgment to begin with God's household; and if it begins with us, what will the outcome be for those who do not obey the gospel of God? And, "If it is hard for the righteous to be saved, what will become of the ungodly and the sinner?"

So then, those who suffer according to God's will should commit themselves to their faithful Creator and continue to do good. 1 Peter 4:12–19

The dynamic interplay between the identity of the believer in the household of God and the interaction of the believer in a hostile culture continues in this summary section. The structure of the letter is indicative of its oral delivery. There are variations on a theme connecting each section and building toward a climax. Peter sets Christian identity and cultural interaction in a full-circle demonstration of faithfulness. Christlike submission and Christlike sacrifice shape the social strategy for subjects, slaves, spouses, and the militant members of God's

A Christ for Culture Strategy

household. Instead of mounting an argumentative defense against an abusive culture, Peter admonishes Christ's followers to respond to the world as Christ did, with humility and gentleness. The believer's arsenal consists of "doing good" and pleasing Christ. Peter envisions a community of resident aliens, chosen outsiders, who establish their identity as the people of God, and for that very reason suffer social hostility.

WHAT CAUSES SUFFERING?

If we embrace Peter's description of the messianic community—own its identity, express its devotion, and practice its obedience—we will suffer. Everyone who finds himself or herself in this picture of costly obedience will resonate with 1 Peter.

Consider the believer who is pursuing a PhD in English literature at a state university. He feels increasingly ostracized as his Christian identity becomes more widely known in the department. His views on metanarrative and reader-response criticism come under harsh criticism by students and professors. He is openly mocked for his biblical views on sexuality and marriage. The tension comes to a head when his advisor, who is gay, pressures him to sleep with him. He refuses, but in doing so jeopardizes his professor's support.

Imagine the believer who is ridiculed by his friends for not smoking pot. He doesn't wish to make a big deal about it, but when pressed, he makes it clear that he doesn't want to get high. But his peers won't let it go. Suspicious that this has something to do with his Christianity, they hound him about it every chance they get and take bets to see who can get him to smoke.

Picture the believer who recently graduated with an MBA and landed a position in a major corporation. She is grateful for her job and likes what she does, but she faces constant pressure to make work her total focus in life. Her colleagues put in unbelievable hours, even coming in regularly on Saturday and Sunday. Her boss makes it clear repeatedly that nothing should come between her and her work if she wants to succeed. When she was hired she explained to her supervisor that she is a Christian and Sunday morning worship is a priority. But he continues to expect her to come into the office on Sunday if they have a project. When she says she can't come in, her supervisor shrugs and says, "Well, that's your decision. Don't blame me if you don't get promoted."

Consider another believer, a police officer who struggles over whether he should attend the bachelor party weekend for one of his non-Christian friends on the force. The expectation of a drunken orgy is all but certain with fellow officers bragging about what they are going to do in Las Vegas. He has no desire to come across "holier than thou" and every intention of supporting his department, but he knows being involved in this bachelor party crosses the line drawn by his faith.

First Peter is relevant for believers in all walks of life and in all professions. It is relevant for the operating room nurse who refuses to participate in late-term abortions. It is relevant for the car mechanic whose employer bills for new parts but uses old replacement parts. It is relevant for the hedge fund investor whose two-million-dollar–end-of-year bonus challenges his kingdom priorities. It is relevant for a mother of three, facing the suburbanite pressure to spend all her time shuttling kids from one activity to another.

To be the faithful presence Christ calls us to be is bound to set us apart as resident aliens, as strangers in our home culture. And even though a Christian may be hardworking, trustworthy, loving, dependable, supportive, and selfless, the world often focuses on the negative differences. As Peter said, "They are surprised that you do not join them in their reckless, wild living, and they heap abuse on you" (1 Pet 4:4).

One of the church's earliest critics was the second-century Greek philosopher Celsus. We know his work through Origen, one of the church's early theologians and apologists. Celsus was especially critical of Christians for their perceived negativity and their critical attitude toward culture. "If all men wanted to be Christians," Celsus wrote, "the Christians would no longer want them."[1] Like a younger sibling who can't stand his older siblings, Celsus complained that Christianity thrived on a negative reaction to the world. If the world was for something, the Christian was against it.

Mirsolav Volf sums up Celsus's argument: "Christian identity is established through the negative activity of setting oneself apart from others. Christian distance from society is a spiteful difference for the sake of difference, nourished by a deep-seated resentment against the dominant social order, which rejected them." Then, Volf asks, "Is this picture what we find in 1 Peter?"[2]

Instead of forging a Christian identity "through a negative process of rejecting the beliefs and practices of others," Volf rightly understands that

1. Chadwick, *Origen*, 133.
2. Volf, *Captive to the Word*, 75.

A Christ for Culture Strategy

1 Peter engages in "a positive process of giving allegiance to something distinctive." "It is significant," Volf writes, "that 1 Peter consistently establishes the difference positively, not negatively. . . . We expect injunctions to reject the ways of the world; instead we find admonitions to follow the path of Christ."[3] First Peter is not a manifesto against the world. Peter shows no interest in condemning the world; his concern is to help the world. The issue for Peter is not how bad the world is, but how good the Christian ought to be. When Peter says, "abstain from sinful desires, which wage war against your soul" (1 Pet 2:11), "the force of the injunction is not 'Do not be as your neighbors are!' but 'Do not be as you were!'"[4]

Nevertheless, the Christian can be all that Peter prays and admonishes us to be and still be subject to Celsus's "Christian-against-the-world" criticism. The world persists in identifying Christ's followers negatively. Nine points of positive agreement, but just one point of disagreement, let's say in the area of sexuality or life's priorities, and the Celsus critique is leveled against the Christian. It is tempting for the gracious believer to be silent or to live in denial on key issues in order to preserve a positive relationships with nonbelievers. Peter understood this dynamic, knowing that a positive Christian identity would provoke a negative reaction from the world and lead to suffering. "Live such good lives among pagans that, though they accuse you of doing wrong, they may see your good deeds and glorify God on the day he visits us" (1 Pet 2:12).

Peter's Christ for culture strategy includes what Christ opposes in our sinful, broken, and fallen human culture, not for the sake of opposition, but for the sake of redemption and reconciliation. David Bentley Hart captures the contrary nature of the gospel, embodied in the people of God and the mission of God, when he writes:

> The Gospel arrived in history as the proclamation of a convulsive disruption *of* history, a genuinely subversive rejection of many of the most venerable cultic, social, and philosophical wisdoms of the ancient world. And the central truth that the Gospel proclaimed —the event as the heart of the event—was the resurrection of Christ, which according to Paul [and Peter] had effectively erased all sacred, social, racial, sexual, and national boundaries, gathered into itself all divine sovereignty over history, and subdued all the

---

3. Ibid., 75.
4. Ibid., 76.

political and spiritual agencies of the cosmos: powers and principalities, thrones and dominions, the 'god of this world.'"[5]

Christ *for* culture underscores the love and compassion that Christ and his followers demonstrate on behalf of a needy culture. "Greater love has no one than this: to lay down one's life for one's friends" (John 15:13). If Christ is *for* culture, who can be against it? The ultimate victory of the risen Lord Jesus Christ is assured, since he has conquered sin and death and overcome the devil and his forces. No one has the power to raise culture up and transform its members but Christ alone. Christ is *for* culture, as Creator, Savior, reigning Lord and coming King.

Suffering rather than success is the key to revealing the true nature of the people of God. Lesslie Newbigin describes the impact of the missional church:

> It follows that the visible embodiment of this new reality is not a movement which will take control of history and shape the future according to its own vision, not a new imperialism, not a victorious crusade. Its visible embodiment will be a community that lives by this story, a community whose existence is visibly defined in the regular rehearsing and reenactment of the story which has given it birth, the story of the self-emptying of God in the ministry, life, death, and resurrection of Jesus.[6]

"DON'T BE SURPRISED"

The previous section concludes with a doxology (1 Pet 4:11) and a new summary section begins with, "Dear friends" (1 Pet 4:12). Peter used this same one-word term of intimacy and endearment (ἀγαπητοί) to begin the main section of his letter (1 Pet 2:11—4:11). "Beloved" underscores the deep bond between fellow believers in Christ even though they had never

---

5. Hart, "No Enduring City," 48. Hart captures the contrariness of the gospel. Kierkegaard agreed: "Christianity is the antithesis to the kingdoms of this world, is heterogeneous, not to be royally authorized is the true thing . . . Christianity is a discommendation . . ." Kierkegaard went on to say, "Persecution, maltreatment, bloodshedding, has by no means done such injury, no, it has been inestimably beneficial in comparison to the radical damage done by official Christianity, which is designed to serve human indolence, mediocrity, by making men believe that indolence, mediocrity and enjoyment of life is Christianity. Do away with official Christianity, let persecution come—that very instant Christianity again exists." Kierkegaard, *Attack Upon 'Christendom,'* 133, 177.

6. Newbigin, *The Gospel in a Pluralist Society*, 120.

met. The apostle prepares the household of God for conflict with the world that they neither sought nor deserved. The messianic community was not looking for a fight. They were not engaged in the culture wars, but in a fight with the sinful desires that wage war against the soul. They were submissive subjects, slaves and spouses, committed to following in Christ's steps. Their concern was to do good and obey the will of God. They sought to show proper respect, keep a clear conscience, and live at peace with everyone. This is the nonthreatening lifestyle that makes suffering shockingly surprising. Why would the culture slander, abuse, ridicule, and mock the very people who seek to do good and cause no harm? Peter warns, "Do not be surprised at the fiery ordeal that has come upon you to test you, as though something strange were happening to you" (1 Pet 4:12).

The "fiery ordeal" comprehends the full range of suffering experienced by Peter's readers and refers back to his initial thought (1 Pet 1:6–7). The purpose of suffering is positive. The fiery process tests the genuineness of the household of God. Peter's image is drawn from the smelting process that refines silver and gold by removing the dross and impurities (Prov 27:21). By using this metaphor at the beginning and the end of the letter he focuses on his theme of suffering for Christ.

Peter's definition of suffering is comprehensive, including "all kinds of trials" (1 Pet 1:6), false accusations (1 Pet 2:12), "ignorant talk of foolish people" (1 Pet 2:15), harsh treatment by superiors (1 Pet 2:18), suffering for doing what is right (1 Pet 3:14), and ridicule for a righteous lifestyle (1 Pet 4:4). Peter does not specify the actual circumstances of the "the fiery ordeal" that came upon them to test them (1 Pet 4:12) nor does he attempt to explain all the ways "your enemy the devil prowls around like a roaring lion looking for someone to devour" (1 Pet 5:8).

As we said earlier, the definition of Christian suffering is not determined by the world's reaction, but by the Christian's response. The "fiery ordeal" can be any experience brought on by an evil, sin-twisted world that calls for a distinctively Christian response. We dare not play Job's counselors in thinking that we can rule out certain trying circumstances as Christian suffering. Suffering, for Peter, is the occasion by which a believer's faith is tested and proven authentic. Suffering is an opportunity for believers to "rejoice" because they "participate in the sufferings of Christ" (1 Pet 4:13). Suffering in the name of Christ is a sign of God's blessing, because "the Spirit of glory and of God rests on you" (1 Pet 4:14).

In some respects Peter's entire letter is commentary on Jesus' eighth Beatitude: "Blessed are those who are persecuted because of righteousness, for theirs is the kingdom of heaven. Blessed are you when people insult you, persecute you and falsely say all kinds of evil against you because of me. Rejoice and be glad, because great is your reward in heaven, for in the same way they persecuted the prophets who were before you" (Matt 5:10–12).

Jesus said, "If the world hates you, keep in mind that it hated me first.... Remember the words I spoke to you: 'No servant is greater than his master.' If they persecuted me, they will persecute you also" (John 15:20). Dietrich Bonhoeffer wrote, "Suffering is the badge of true discipleship," but many Christians seem to think that success is the sign of God's blessing.[7] Jesus did not promise the messianic community peace and prosperity; he promised peace in the midst of persecution and suffering. In fact he said, "Woe to you when all people speak well of you, for that is how their fathers treated the false prophets" (Luke 6:26). "Since all the beatitudes describe what every Christian disciple is intended to be," writes John Stott, "we conclude that the condition of being despised and rejected, slandered and persecuted, is as much a normal mark of Christian discipleship as being pure in heart or merciful."[8] "The fellowship of the beatitudes is the fellowship of the Crucified. With him it has lost all, and with him it has found all."[9] The Apostle Paul put it simply when he said, "Everyone who wants to live a godly life in Christ Jesus will be persecuted" (2 Tim 3:12).

Lesslie Newbigin explains why the messianic community receives the negative response that it often does, even when believers follow Christ's example and lead with goodness. The great paradox confronting the church is that this gospel of peace in Christ that is designed to destroy the walls of hostility actually provokes hostility. The old paganisms and the new messianisms fight against the church with everything they have. Newbigin writes,

> Wherever the gospel is preached, new ideologies appear—secular humanism, nationalism, Marxism—movements which offer the vision of new age, an age freed from all the ills that beset human life, freed from hunger and disease and war—on other terms.
>
> Once the gospel is preached and there is a community which lives by the gospel, then the question of the ultimate meaning of

---

7. Bonhoeffer, *Cost of Discipleship*, 100.
8. Stott, *Christian Counter-Culture*, 53.
9. Bonhoeffer, *Cost of Discipleship*, 127.

history is posed and other messiahs appear. So the crisis of history is deepened. Even more significant as an example of this development than the rise of Marxism is the rise of Islam. Islam, which means simply submission, is the mightiest of all the post-Christian movements which claim to offer the kingdom of God without the cross. The denial of the crucifixion is and must always be central to Islamic teaching.[10]

The gospel doesn't write the culture off. We cannot wash our hands of the whole mess, and go about being nice to our friends and living a nice Christian life. Nor does the gospel permit us to become one with the culture, enmeshed in a live-and-let-live ethos that is at its root antichrist. The challenge for the household of God is to "relate to the world within a dialectic of affirmation and antithesis."[11] We are called to engage the world in a way that is a true benefit to the world. In the Spirit, we are empowered to have a prophetic, fruitful, and insightful witness.

Instead of opting for the strategies of worldly power, which involve coercion, exploitation, and propaganda, Peter calls believers to make "other types of power imaginable."[12] Following the example of their crucified Lord, the people of God operate with a "fundamentally different kind of social power."[13] Ordinary believers in their ordinary lives are called to take after Jesus in the world. This will inevitably lead to suffering. To think otherwise leads to the kind of blindsided attack that Peter warns believers to guard against. "Don't be surprised! . . . But rejoice inasmuch as you participate in the sufferings of Christ, so that you may be overjoyed when his glory is revealed" (1 Pet 4:12–13).

SUFFERING FOR THE WRONG REASONS

"If you suffer," Peter says, "it should not be as a murderer or thief or any other kind of criminal, or even as a meddler" (1 Pet 4:15). Vinay Samuel, director of the International Fellowship of Evangelical Mission Theologians, defines religious fanatics as those who "feel called to take the world

---

10. Newbigin, *The Gospel in a Pluralist Society*, 122
11. Hunter, *To Change the World*, 231.
12. Ibid., 186.
13. Ibid., 188.

by its neck and conform it to their vision of what the world should be like. To do that, they will sacrifice everything, including themselves."[14]

An extreme example of a religious fanatic is former Presbyterian minister Paul Hill, who murdered a doctor and his bodyguard because the doctor performed abortions. Right up to his execution Hill remained defiant and unrepentant. He said, "I believe the state, by executing me, will be making me a martyr."[15] Not unlike an al-Qaeda suicide bomber, Paul Hill died in vain. The religious fanatic refuses to see the difference between murder and martyrdom—between committing a hate crime and seeking social justice. In the name of righteousness he rejects Christ's righteousness. Instead of submitting to the will of God, he asserts his own will. His cause is absolute and he is willing to sacrifice all things, including himself and the will of God.

It is unlikely that Peter's readers were tempted to kill or steal or commit a crime for the sake of the gospel. If they were his letter might have taken a very different focus. Peter framed the issue in a manner similar to the way Jesus framed the sixth commandment in the Sermon on the Mount (Matt 5:21–22). Probably no one in the original Sermon on the Mount audience had committed murder, but they had insulted their brother or sister. Until Jesus, no one had ever related murder to everyday insults and name-calling. Like the Master, Peter linked the worse crimes, that no Christian would think of committing, to the overlooked and seemingly acceptable behavior of meddling.

The word *meddler* (ἀλλοτριεπίσκοπος) appears to be unique to Peter. It combines "overseer" and "strange" to describe a person who gets involved in affairs that are none of his business.[16] He is a "busybody," meddling in other people's concerns. The Apostle Paul may have expressed a similar warning, although he didn't use this word, when he said, "Make it your ambition to lead a quiet life: You should mind your own business and work with your hands, just as we told you, so that your daily life may win the respect of outsiders and so that you will not be dependent on anybody" (1 Thess 4:11–12).

Peter's focus was on how believers interface with the world negatively. Meddling describes an ineffective and bothersome approach to the world that sets the cause of Christ back even though it may advance a religious

---

14. Samuel, "Religion: Cause or Cure for Terrorism?," 10.
15. ITV News, "Abortion activist defiant in death."
16. Elliott, *1 Peter*, 786.

A Christ for Culture Strategy

agenda. This meddling may have included "censuring the behavior of outsiders on the basis of claims to a higher morality, interfering with family relationships, fomenting domestic discontent and discord, or tactless attempts at conversion."[17]

Instead of blaming the world for being bad, Peter wanted believers to impress the world with God's goodness. He wanted Christ's followers to give the world the reason for the hope they had in Christ. His warning against meddling challenges the believers' approach to culture. Some ministries make a habit of playing on the fears of believers by describing how evil and depraved the culture is. This strategy may raise funds and energize emotional support, but it contradicts the New Testament. Paul said, "What business is it of mine to judge those outside the church? Are you not to judge those inside? God will judge those outside" (1 Cor 5:12). Peter knew how foolish it was to try to bully the world into conformity to Christian morality. Christians who base their public appeal on what they hate about the culture rather than on the life-transforming good news of Jesus Christ should not think that their suffering is for Christ's sake.

A FAITHFUL PRESENCE

"If you suffer as a Christian, do not be ashamed, but praise God that you bear his name" (1 Pet 4:16). The label *Christian* (Χριστιανός) only occurs in the Bible here and twice in Acts (Acts 11:26; 26:28). It is thought to be a derogatory reference to Christ's followers, along the lines of "Christ-lackeys."[18] If the world intends to shame you, Peter insists, "do not be ashamed." Suffering because you bear the name of Christ is reason enough to praise God.

The apostles found in the name of Christ a direct link to the reality of God. Jesus Christ not only embodied the message of God but also revealed the character of God. His name became synonymous with God himself. Therefore, to be called by his name involved an inseparable commitment to a patterning after his life and a confession of his being. In the minds of the apostles the name of Christ was an all-encompassing expression representing the totality of Jesus' earthly ministry as well as the reality of the glorified state of the risen Christ. The "name" was shorthand for everything that Jesus meant to them—so much so that on occasion they referred simply to "the Name" (Acts 5:41; 3 John 7).

17. Ibid., 788.
18. Ibid., 791.

"For it is time for judgment to begin with God's household" (1 Pet 4:17). The "fiery ordeal" sorts out the true followers of Christ from the fakes and serves as preliminary to the final judgment. Peter says in effect, "Don't worry about the world, the world will worry about itself. Be concerned about the household of God." Peter makes a case for focusing on the holiness and faithfulness of the household of God. Instead of trying to change the world, be the people of God.

Instead of worrying about what the world thinks, instead of growing angry about what the world does, be concerned about living according to God's will. Instead of lamenting the increasing numbers of sexually active teens, cohabiting adults, and abortions in the culture at large, commit yourself to practicing biblical sexuality in the body of Christ. We truly have our hands full "purifying" ourselves "by obeying the truth" (1 Pet 1:22). If the "holy nation" spent more time ridding itself of "all malice and all deceit, hypocrisy, envy, and slander" (1 Pet 2:1) then it might have a far greater impact on the nations.

"And if it begins with us, what will the outcome be for those who do not obey the gospel of God?" (1 Pet 4:17). Peter is under no illusion that this will be easy, but it makes a whole lot more sense for the people of God to practice the will of God than to fixate on the fact that the world doesn't. If Christians are a mirror image of the culture, why would the world ask us about the reason for the hope we have? If half our marriages end in divorce and if our children lose their faith in university, why would the world look to the church for hope?

Peter underscored the challenge with a quote from Proverbs: "If it is hard for the righteous to be saved, what will become of the ungodly and the sinner?" (Prov 11:31). Invariably when Peter quotes from the Old Testament he "consistently preserves the original context," and this quotation is true to form.[19] The proverbs that surround Peter's quote focus on this topic and add to his emphasis: "The fruit of the righteous is a tree of life, and the one who is wise saves lives" (Prov 11:30). "Whoever loves discipline loves knowledge, but whoever hates correction is stupid" (Prov 12:1).

Silas may have drawn out this added emphasis as he discussed this with various groups of believers scattered throughout Asia Minor. What is clear is that Peter's stress corresponds to the Master's emphasis. Jesus said in the Sermon on the Mount, "Not everyone who says to me, 'Lord, Lord,' will enter the kingdom of heaven, but only the one who does the will of my

---

19. Jobes, *1 Peter*, 292.

A Christ for Culture Strategy

Father who is in heaven" (Matt 7:21). Peter's concern was this: "Will the insults, abuse, ostracism, and even more serious and threatening pressures drive them to deny Christ, renounce their faith, and return to pagan beliefs and living, thus rejecting the gospel of God as surely as those who never made a profession?"[20]

Those who suffer "according to God's will" (1 Pet 4:19) determine to entrust themselves to God's care and seek to practice his goodness no matter what happens. Instead of feeling condemned by the world or even abandoned by God, believers are challenged to "commit themselves to their faithful Creator and continue to do good" (1 Pet 4:19). Peter reminds believers everywhere that they have the home-field advantage. They may not feel at home in this world, but this is their Father's world and the key to human flourishing belongs to their faithful Creator.

> This is my Father's world, O let me not forget,
> That though the wrong seems oft so strong, God is the ruler yet.
> This is my Father's world: the battle is not done;
> Jesus who died shall be satisfied, and earth and heav'n be one.

---

20. Ibid., 294.

11

Good Shepherds

To the elders among you, I appeal as a fellow elder and a witness of Christ's sufferings who also will share in the glory to be revealed: Be shepherds of God's flock that is under your care, watching over them—not because you must, but because you are willing, as God wants you to be; not pursuing dishonest gain, but eager to serve; not lording it over those entrusted to you, but being examples to the flock. And when the Chief Shepherd appears, you will receive the crown of glory that will never fade away. 1 Peter 5:1–4

Peter's spiritual direction moves seamlessly from social opposition in the culture to relational concerns in the household of God. Peter has consistently shifted from external conditions to internal dynamics.[1] This synergy between two force fields gives a realistic appraisal of the challenges and benefits facing Christ's followers. Cross-bearing humility is the strategy for relating to culture and Christlike humility is essential for the household of God. Social hostility and its ugly features of envy, competition, coercion, intimidation, and slander must not be allowed to impact the internal dynamic of the messianic community. The people of God cannot afford to let the pressure of the world corrupt their behavior in the household of faith.[2]

Peter has avoided the word "church," presumably to distance the messianic community from any comparison to other institutional assemblies.

---

1 Achtemeier, *1 Peter*, 321.

2. Harink, *1 and 2 Peter*, 120.

There is little implied organizational structure and no hierarchical official leadership. Peter's focus has been on the familial household, reminding believers to "love one another deeply, from the heart" (1 Pet 1:22), to get rid of "all malice and all deceit," to "crave pure spiritual milk" (1 Pet 2:2), to be like-minded, sympathetic, loving, compassionate, and humble (1 Pet 3:8), and finally, "above all, [to] love each other deeply" (1 Pet 4:8). Believers face two challenges: living in the family of God and living in an alien and hostile culture. Peter integrates theology and ethics in a manner that has intellectual depth, practical relevance, and personal impact.

His pastoral letter exudes humility and models the love and respect shepherds need for God's flock. Peter has waited to address "the elders" (πρεσβυτέρους). Everything he has said up until now applies to all believers. There is little difference between ordinary believers and elders when it comes to obedience, holiness, devotion, and sacrifice. All believers are called to salvation, service, sacrifice, and simplicity. There are no elite saints who sign on for a "second blessing" or who follow "the counsels of perfection." Peter only knows one form of spiritual maturity, which he illustrates by highlighting faithful slaves and wives. He offers a bottom-up profile of the true disciple. There is no greater gift given than the gift of the "new birth into a living hope through the resurrection of Jesus Christ" and no higher status than being heir to the gracious gift of life (1 Pet 1:3; 3:7).

CO-ELDERS

Peter uses the first-person singular sparingly, only three times in the entire letter. Twice he uses it to signal a fresh exhortation: "Dear friends, I urge you (παρακαλῶ), as foreigners and exiles, to abstain from sinful desires . . ." (1 Pet 2:11); "To the elders among you, I appeal (παρακαλῶ) as a fellow elder . . ." (1 Pet 5:1).[3] The third time comes at the end when he commends Silas, "whom I regard as a faithful brother" (1 Pet 5:12). From the outset, Peter's apostolic authority is implicit. He speaks boldly, but he doesn't throw his weight around. He has neither beguiled his readers nor bullied them. His exhortation is direct and personal, not dogmatic, firmly rooted in the Old Testament and in the testimony of Jesus.

---

3. Elliott writes, "Ranging in tone between a request and a command, it serves to establish the proper diplomatic atmosphere for the author's exhortation of his fellow-elders with remarks that are both directive and reassuring." Elliott, *1 Peter*, 816.

His appeal to the elders rests on a threefold identification: their shared responsibility, their shared experience, and their shared glory. He describes himself as a co-elder (συμπρσβύτερος), a word he may have coined to emphasize their coworking relationship.[4] Peter sees himself as a peer, not a superior; as a brother, not an official. Although he is an apostle, he does not pull rank. He is one with them in the responsibility of shepherding the household of faith. Whatever authority he and his fellow elders have comes from Christ. Along with them, he is a witness of Christ's sufferings. The word for witness (μάρτυς) can refer to an eyewitness account or to the act of bearing witness. Peter may have intended a double meaning. As an apostle he was an eyewitness of the sufferings of Christ, and as an elder he bears witness to the sufferings of Christ.[5]

Finally, Peter shares their anticipation of the glory to be revealed. Christ's suffering and glory are understood together. To speak of Christ's sufferings is to affirm "the glories that would follow" (1 Pet 1:11). Christ's followers participate in his sufferings, so that they "may be overjoyed when his glory is revealed" (1 Pet 4:13). Peter is quick to give Christ's passion eschatological perspective. Divine vindication is imminent. The end result of the refining process is "praise, glory and honor when Jesus Christ is revealed" (1 Pet 1:7).[6]

SHEPHERDS OF GOD'S FLOCK

Peter's brief word to elders comes *after* he has made his theological and ethical case for the household of God. His primary exhortation has been to his "dear friends" to whom he has made his case for salvation (1 Pet 1:1–12), sanctification (1 Pet 1:13–2:3), solidarity (1 Pet 2:4–10), submission (1 Pet 2:11–3:7), and suffering (1 Pet 3:8–4:19). His spiritual direction integrates evangelism and edification. He offers a strategy for engaging a

---

4. Ibid., 817.

5. Achtemeier disagrees. He writes, "While the phrase . . . can be construed to mean an eyewitness to Christ's crucifixion . . . the unanimous gospel tradition that Peter was in fact not present at the crucifixion cuts directly across any such construal." Achtemeier, *1 Peter*, 323. But if Christ's passion includes the road to the cross, along with Gethsemane, the beatings, and the trial, Peter qualifies as an eyewitness of Christ's sufferings.

6. Peter's threefold identification with his co-elders recalls the Apostle John's description in Revelation: "I, John, your brother and companion in the suffering and kingdom and patient endurance that are ours in Jesus . . ." (Rev 1:9). Like Peter, John stresses solidarity, not status; partnership, not position; and suffering, not power.

hostile culture and experiencing joy in the messianic community that is rooted in the example and empowerment of Jesus Christ. To that full picture he now brings a word of exhortation to the shepherds of God's flock, who serve under the Chief Shepherd, Jesus Christ.

Peter begins with an imperative, *be shepherds* (1 Pet 5:2). The pastoral image implies responsibility, rather than a proud position symbolizing authority. In some religious circles, pastors can be called "shepherds" or "archbishops" and it makes no difference. The meaning is the same. But when Peter used the metaphor the meaning was still fresh and true to its biblical heritage. Shepherding invokes a rich history of biblical meaning stretching from Abraham to Jesus. Peter's rural readers identified with the earthy image of the shepherd. The metaphor had not yet been corrupted by priests calling themselves shepherds, dressed in chasubles and dalmatics, carrying a golden staff. Before the confusion of images, shepherds were working-class laborers who gathered, guided, and protected their flocks.

Peter reiterates the God-centered nature of shepherding in three ways. First, shepherds are entrusted with a flock that belongs to God, not themselves. Their work is always a matter of stewardship, not ownership. Pastors who refer to "my people" ought to be mindful that the people belong to God and God alone. Second, the willingness to do the work of shepherding is inspired and instructed by the will of God, not by an ambitious ego or a needy personality. The appearance of godliness is no substitute for the power of God (2 Tim 3:5) and a reputation for zeal, apart from the will of God, is worthless (Rom 10:2). Faith in Jesus and the faith of Jesus are inseparable. Whatever is done in the name of Jesus is to be done the Jesus way. Third, all shepherds serve under the Chief Shepherd and their reward comes when Christ appears. Once again, Peter draws out the eschatological perspective. He completes this triad of divine identification, God's flock, God's will, and God's glory, in a way that corresponds to his triad of solidarity, coworker, cowitness, and corecipient of "the glory to be revealed" (1 Pet 5:1, 4).

Peter composes his brief exhortation to co-elders with considerable care. He weaves three triads together, including their shared solidarity, divine identification, and work ethic. He qualifies the shepherds' responsibility to watch over God's flock in a threefold negative/positive tension: (1) "not because you must, but because you are willing . . ." (1 Pet 5:2); (2) "not pursuing dishonest gain, but eager to serve . . ." (1 Pet 5:2); (3) "not lording it over those entrusted to you, but [as] examples to the flock" (1 Pet 5:3).

THE PASSIVE FLOCK

Our various traditions may make it difficult for us to hear what Peter is saying about shepherding.[7] The Reformation went a long way in correcting the unbiblical notion of the sacerdotal priesthood, but the distinction between pastor and people remains troublesome. Instead of an ontological or mystical superiority, there is now a functional superiority. The difference between the shepherd and his flock is not between "rational and irrational creatures" but between conscientious parent and infant child.[8] In *The Reformed Pastor*, Richard Baxter, the seventeenth-century Anglican, reinforced the notion of the active pastor and the passive flock.

Baxter stressed "that every flock should have its own pastor, and every pastor its own flock." Instead of entrusting a ministry team with the task of oversight, Baxter saw a single pastor exercising oversight over a particular congregation. "From this relation of pastor and flock, arise all the duties which they mutually owe to each other."[9] Baxter acknowledged the burden of this responsibility and advised that congregations ought to be kept small enough for pastors to fulfill their duties. "God will not lay upon us natural impossibilities: he will not bind men to leap up to the moon, to touch the stars, or to number the sands of the sea."[10]

Again, Baxter's proposed solution to these "natural impossibilities" was not every-member ministry, the gifts of the Spirit, and the priesthood

---

7. The biblical imagery of the shepherd and the flock has been misconstrued. Tradition has reinforced the notion that the shepherd is actively in charge and the flock is passively submissive. In Catholic tradition, ordination conferred supernatural power on the priest, rendering him far superior to ordinary believers. In his description of the relationship between pastor and people, John Chrysostom seemed to take the imagery of the shepherd and the flock literally. Those entrusted with the care of souls must surpass all others and soar above them in excellence of spirit. Women and most men were ineligible for such a high calling. "Let all womankind give way before the magnitude of the task—and indeed most men. Bring before us those who far excel all others. . . . Let the difference between shepherd and sheep be as great as the distinction between rational and irrational creatures, not to say even more, since matters of much greater moment are at stake." The dignity of pastors was so exalted that it was as "though they were already translated to heaven and had transcended human nature and were freed from our passions." John Chrysostom viewed the superiority of the pastor over his flock in almost ontological terms: the very being of the priest was on an altogether different plane than mere mortals. Chrysostom, *On the Priesthood*, 54.

8. Ibid, 40.

9. Baxter, *The Reformed Pastor*, 88.

10. Ibid., 88.

of all believers, but smaller congregations. He wrote, "If the pastoral office consists in overseeing all the flock, then surely the number of souls under the care of each pastor must not be greater than he is able to take such heed to as is here required."[11] Baxter warned that God would require the blood of so many parishes at the hands of bishops who tried to do too much. Nor was he impressed with pastors who gave themselves to preaching and let others carry out the work of pastoral care on the flock. Baxter called for the pastor to know the spiritual condition of every person under his charge. "Does not a careful shepherd look after every individual sheep?"[12] Baxter was not adverse to hiring ministerial assistants to share oversight responsibilities, and advised pastors to cut their salaries if necessary to do so. Apparently, it never occurred to him that the body was gifted by the Spirit to look after itself. Instead of every-member ministry, Baxter envisioned a single minister ministering to a flock small enough so that the pastor knew everyone personally.

Apparently Baxter did not realize that the very humility he called for as an essential remedy to the sin of pride required redefining his pastoral theology and correcting his overemphasis on the solo responsibilities of the pastor.

"The only serious problem with Baxter's classic," writes George Hunter, "is its major assumption. When Baxter wrote, the Christian priesthood had already modeled vocational narcissism for over a millennium. With clear exceptions, including monarchs, politicians, rock stars, super-jocks, and supermodels, priests have exceeded most other vocations in the degree to which they have assumed that the world revolves around what they do."[13]

George Hunter argues that Baxter's daunting job description of the pastor has persisted in the popular imagination of most Protestants. The pastor is called to serve "as every person's evangelist, catechist, teacher, overseer, counselor, disciplinarian, liturgist, and preacher." He must also minister to the sick, visit from house to house, and preside at weddings and funerals. For the most part, laypeople "are essentially spectators," or at best, third-string players waiting for the chance to serve when the ordained minister is unable to perform his duties.[14]

---

11. Ibid., 88.
12. Ibid., 91.
13. Hunter, *Radical Outreach*, 106.
14. Ibid., 105–7.

For Baxter the metaphor of the flock is an apt description of a docile, needy congregation, dependent on the pastor for guidance and correction. By the time he refers to 1 Peter 2:9, he seems blinded to the implications of the priesthood of all believers. Baxter uses the description of the church as "a chosen generation, a royal priesthood, a holy nation, a peculiar people" (1 Pet 2:9) as an incentive for pastors to be diligent in their work and not to neglect these valuable yet needy people. Baxter writes, "What a high honor it is to be but one of them, yes, but a door-keeper in the house of God! But to be the priest of these priests, and the ruler of these kings—this is such an honor as multiplies your obligations to diligence and fidelity in so noble an employment."[15]

ONE-MAN SHOW

Shepherding is not a one-man show. Most pastors at some point in their ministry have had to deal with these conventional expectations. It never seems to fail that a few lay leaders see it as their responsibility to hold their pastor accountable for living up to a Baxter-style pastoral job description. Pastors often feel like failures because they cannot satisfy the excessive demands and burdens placed upon them.

In an institutional church setting, it is not easy to distinguish between obligatory employment duties and true biblical responsibilities. Regrettably, many pastors find their work all-consuming. They have lost the joy of serving because they have labored long and hard under a burden of false expectations that drive the pastoral job description. It is as if all of a doctor's patients knew one another and they all got together weekly to compare notes. What if all the clients of a lawyer enjoyed potluck suppers together? Imagine the solidarity and synergy of demand; the oppressive nature of accountability; the peculiar power of shared complaints and expectations.

Many subscribe to a philosophy of ministry that demands that the pastor be all things to all people at all times, cheerfully! The doctor-patient relationship is professionally limited to the physical needs of the patient. You wouldn't think of calling your doctor because you couldn't afford to get your car fixed. Imagine showing up at your doctor's office just to spend some time together because you don't feel your doctor knows you very well. The attorney-client relationship is usually limited to the client's legal needs. Lawyers don't usually attend their client's birthday parties, wedding

---

15. Baxter, *The Reformed Pastor*, 131.

anniversaries, piano recitals, or listen to them as they graphically recount their visit to the doctor, unless of course they are suing their doctor for malpractice. But many churchgoers feel there is nothing that their pastor should not be interested in about their lives, because he is their pastor. He must be interested in them and everything about them. How can a pastor have a one-on-one relationship with several hundred members and remain sane? But many parishioners believe that this is a reasonable expectation. Many pastors suffer from unrelenting guilt for disappointing their parishioners' expectations.

"Not because you must, but because you are willing" (1 Pet 5:2). Unless there is a plurality of serving elders in the household of God and a shared understanding of the priesthood of all believers, there is little hope for pastors to sustain a willing spirit. The joy of ministry will dissipate over time because of unbiblical and unreasonable expectations. Under the burden of an unrelenting job description many pastors wonder why they no longer enjoy watching over God's flock. Their "willingness" to serve is not in line with God's will and they feel worse than obligated; they feel trapped.

"Not pursuing dishonest gain, but eager to serve" (1 Pet 5:2). Since many of today's pastoral obligations are driven more by a consumer mentality than spiritual maturity, pastors are tempted to compensate themselves for the annoyances, pressures, and troubles of their work. When elders are isolated and estranged from their true calling, biblical shepherding, they are more easily tempted to pursue "dishonest gain." Money becomes a compensating calculation, offsetting the frustration they feel for playing along in the Jesus business. I can't help but feel that Judas became so discouraged over his investment in Jesus' ministry that he was determined to get something out of it. Rather than walking away with nothing, he had his thirty pieces of silver. What a tragedy! But this pathetic dynamic is played out much more often than we may realize. The positive counterpoint to the giving-getting malady is simply stated: be "eager to serve." The first four chapters of 1 Peter serve as a great teaching guide for meaningful service. Instead of meeting market-driven felt needs, Peter challenges his fellow elders to encourage the people of God in their Trinitarian identity, cruciform lifestyle, and their deep love for one another.

"Not lording it over those entrusted to you, but [be] examples to the flock" (1 Pet 5:3). Peter warns his co-elders against spiritual malpractice. It is easy to see how these three negative elements—distasteful duty, dishonest gain, and domination—coalesce to form a leadership that sabotages the gospel and paves the way for social accommodation. Peter's concern echoes the Master's perspective given just before Holy Week: "You know that the rulers of the Gentiles lord it over them, and their high officials exercise authority over them. Not so with you. Instead, whoever wants to become great among you must be your servant, and whoever wants to be first must be your slave—just as the Son of Man did not come to be served, but to serve, and to give his life as a ransom for many" (Matt 20:25-28).

The way to shepherd is to be an example to the flock. Don't "bossily tell others what to do, tenderly show them the way" (1 Pet 5:3, *The Message*). Good shepherds take after the Good Shepherd who "lays down his life for the sheep" (John 10:11). Peter's advice here is consistent with what he said earlier, "To this you were called, because Christ suffered for you, leaving you an example, that you should follow in his steps" (1 Pet 2:21).

The New Testament shows little interest in how churches arranged and organized their leadership offices. We know that the "organization" of the early church was simple, shared, and highly relational.[16] Ironically, the modern church is much more top down and male oriented than the early church. Michael Green observes in *Evangelism in the Early Church* that Christianity "was from its inception a lay movement, and so it continued for a remarkably long time." When the believers were evicted from Jerusalem as a result of persecution which followed Stephen's martyrdom, men and women, "went everywhere gossiping the gospel; they did it naturally, enthusiastically, and with the conviction of those who are not paid to say

---

16. Walter Liefeld makes the following observations on the organization and structure of the early church: (1) house churches with plural leadership by elders kept the organization relatively simple; (2) there is no evidence in the New Testament that one person with special authorization "presided" at the Lord's Supper; (3) the interdependence of ministry and leadership was stressed (each needs the other); (4) no provision was made in the New Testament for apostolic succession; (5) pastors functioned within congregations, not above them; (6) there were no certain definitions of their role or rank; (7) elders were shepherds, not a board of directors; (8) ordination as we know it was not practiced in the early church. The laying on of hands conferred a "gift," not a status. It was not an "office" or "position" but a gift "in" the person to enable him to minister; (9) Jesus discouraged the use of titles to portray superiority or authority (Matt 23:8). By contrast, today's perceptions of leadership and organizational complexity have tended to discourage shared service and every-member ministry. Liefeld observes: (1) ministry responsibilities are formalized into "offices" and ordination "elevates the individual and bestows privileges not envisioned in the New Testament"; (2) the authority of the apostles has been transferred to today's pastors; (3) healthy servant leadership teaching and guidance is not sufficiently distinguished from unhealthy domineering teaching and leadership; (4) women have been marginalized and their ministry role downplayed. Liefeld, "The Nature of Authority in the New Testament," 255-71.

that sort of thing. Consequently, they were taken seriously, and the movement spread, notably among the lower classes." The absence of a distinction between "full-time ministers and laymen in this responsibility to spread the gospel by every means possible" meant that "there was equally no distinction between the sexes in the matter. . . . Everyone was to be an apologist, at least to the extent of being ready to give a good account of the hope that was within them. And this emphatically included women. They had a very large part to play in the advance of Christianity."[17]

SILAS'S PREACHING

It is not difficult to imagine Silas expounding on the biblical imagery of the shepherd. He traveled all the way from Rome to encourage the "resident aliens" of Asia Minor. His hosts were undoubtedly hungry for good preaching. Maybe not a three-point sermon from a pulpit, but a solid biblical exposition around the table. I picture Silas presenting Psalm 23 as a significant description of pastoral care. The psalmist builds on the foundational truth: "the Lord is my shepherd."[18] Our understanding of who a pastor is and what a pastor does begins here. This is important because if the Lord is not our shepherd—our pastor—then no human pastor will ever make a very good pastor for us. No pastor will ever become a satisfying substitute for the Lord, no matter how hard he or she tries.

Silas ruled out the possibility of Christ's followers living vicariously through their pastor. The notion that pastors can substitute and symbolize the life of faith for lazy parishioners would have been thrown out. No one can ever say, "Pastor so-and-so is my shepherd, I lack nothing." If the Lord is our shepherd—our pastor—we have everything we need. The Chief Shepherd provides:

> 1. Rest and provision for life: "He makes me lie down in green pastures, he leads me beside quiet waters, he refreshes my soul" (Ps 23:2–3).

17. Green, *Evangelism in the Early Church*, 173–75.

18. The word *shepherd* translates into Latin as *pastor*, from which we get our English word *pastor*. Originally it meant "feeder" or "giver of pasture." Since Jesus identified himself as the Good Shepherd in the Gospel of John, all who follow him as the risen Lord cannot help but think of him as our shepherd when we read this psalm. Psalm 23:1, "The Lord is my shepherd," bears the force of Psalm 110:1, "The Lord says to my Lord: 'Sit at my right hand until I make your enemies a footstool for your feet.'" Both psalms are messianic psalms. David, the shepherd-king, acknowledged that the Lord was his Shepherd.

2. Guidance in righteousness: "He guides me along the right paths for his name's sake" (Ps 23:3).

3. Comfort in crisis: "Even though I walk through the deepest, darkest valley, I will fear no evil, for you are with me; your rod and your staff they comfort me" (Ps 23:4).

4. Fellowship and protection through hospitality: "You prepare a table before me in the presence of my enemies" (Ps 23:5).

5. Affirmation for significant work: "You anoint my head with oil; my cup overflows" (Ps 23:5).

6. Goodness in providence: "Surely goodness and love will follow me all the days of my life" (Ps 23:6).

7. Everlasting security in community and worship: "And I will dwell in the house of the Lord forever" (Ps 23:6).

When we say, "the Lord is my shepherd, I shall not want," we acknowledge that our primary source of rest, guidance, comfort, fellowship, significance, goodness, and security is the Lord. Pastors make poor substitutes for the Lord, but they make great shepherds if they keep pointing us to the Lord. Their job is to guide us to the Good Shepherd. From these seven provisions we can build a model of what a pastor does and what a congregation should expect in a pastor. The picture is not so ideal as to be unreal and each of these attributes of care is essential.

Congregations can be saved a lot of wear and tear if they are led by pastors who refuse to substitute their agenda or religious programming for the rest and nourishment found in the Lord. "Be still and know that I am God" (Ps 46:10) will always be more important than the elders' "five-year plan." A church guided "for his name's sake" (Ps 23:3) will not be guided by the pastor's ego, but by the Lord's authority. The word of God, and not the spirit of the times, will determine the right paths to take. Someone in the household of God is always in the deepest, darkest valley. Pastors cannot absorb this pain as if it were their own and expect to serve the body. They are little help if they try to live vicariously through the suffering and trauma of individual believers. Their responsibility is to say to a brother or sister who is going through the deepest, darkest valley, "The Lord is our comfort, we will fear no evil" (Ps 23:4).

When pastors lead worship at holy communion, the congregation is reminded that only the Lord can set this table in the presence of evil. It is the Lord's body that was broken and it is his blood that was poured out, not the pastor's. Only the Lord saves and redeems. Pastors might wish they could anoint, designate, call, and empower, but that's not their calling; it is the Lord's. Pastors have their limits. They might wish they could make people's cup overflow, but they can't. Only the Lord can do that. Even the elders who willingly watch over the flock, who eagerly serve, and who endeavor to be an example to God's flock will falter and fail. There is not a pastor around who does not regularly disappoint. But if the Lord is our shepherd we shall not want.

Silas instructed these outposts of hope to look to the crucified and risen Christ as their Chief Shepherd. Co-elders share in the shepherding responsibility of the household of God, but it is not up to them to shape believers around their hopes and dreams. It is the Lord's house, not theirs. And the rest, guidance, comfort, fellowship, significance, goodness, and security that we all need comes from Christ alone. Only then can we say, *The Lord is our pastor, we shall not want.*

FEED MY SHEEP

It is difficult to imagine Silas not sharing the story of Peter's encounter with the risen Lord. Surely the account of John 21 provided context for Peter's spiritual direction on shepherding. Jesus did not say to Peter, "Lead an army," or "Launch a crusade," or "Compete with Rome." Jesus didn't even say, "Build my kingdom." He said, "Feed my sheep" (John 21:15–19). Peter was not given a vision of heroic service, only the long-suffering, persevering, pastoral care responsibilities required of the shepherd. The sheep are in need of feeding, not herding; tending, not catering.

Peter's personal story line fits well with his letter's spiritual direction. Peter accepted the challenge and identified with God's interests. To borrow the words of Oswald Chambers, the Lord says in effect, "Identify yourself with My interests in other people," not "Identify Me with your interests in other people."[19] After many years Peter was still feeding Christ's sheep, tending to the chosen outsiders scattered throughout Asia Minor. He embraced the principle of the cross, "my life for yours," and encouraged others to do the same. "Dear friends, do not be surprised at the painful trial you are suffering, as though something strange were happening to you. But rejoice that you participate in the sufferings of Christ, so that you may be overjoyed when his glory is revealed" (1 Pet 4:12). Silas was there to testify that Peter practiced what he preached.

19. Chambers, *My Utmost For His Highest*, 292.

12

Humility

> *In the same way, you who are younger, submit yourselves to your elders. All of you, clothe yourselves with humility toward one another, because "God opposes the proud but shows favor to the humble." Humble yourselves, therefore, under God's mighty hand, that he may lift you up in due time. Cast all your anxiety on him because he cares for you.*
>
> *Be alert and of sober mind. Your enemy the devil prowls around like a roaring lion looking for someone to devour. Resist him, standing firm in the faith, because you know that the family of believers throughout the world is undergoing the same kind of sufferings.*
>
> *And the God of all grace, who called you to his eternal glory in Christ, after you have suffered a little while, will himself restore you and make you strong, firm, and steadfast. To him be the power for ever and ever. Amen.*
>
> *With the help of Silas, whom I regard as a faithful brother, I have written to you briefly, encouraging you and testifying that this is the true grace of God. Stand fast in it. She who is in Babylon, chosen together with you, sends you her greetings, and so does my son Mark. Greet one another with a kiss of love. Peace to all of you who are in Christ.* 1 Peter 5:5–14

Humility may not impress us as the strategic mind-set for the people of God, but Peter thought so. He had his eye on the "weaker" members of the household of God, who by their Christlike lifestyles proved the power of the gospel. His outposts of hope produced a quiet revolution. The advance of the gospel rested on ordinary believers who followed in the steps of Christ. They were the ones prepared to give an answer for the hope they had in Christ.

"Guidance" is a better word than "leadership" in the relational setting of the household of God. The emphasis is kept where it belongs: on worship, obedience, and mission. The team of co-elders *bears responsibility*, rather than *holds rank*, for the well-being and spiritual growth of the messianic community. Suffering is Peter's major concern. He plants the cross of Christ in every section of his letter as the redemptive foundation and mission motivation for suffering "grief in all kinds of trials" (1 Pet 1:6) and "keeping a clear conscience, so that those who speak maliciously against your good behavior in Christ may be ashamed of their slander" (1 Pet 3:16).

Peter adds the younger generation to his bottom-up profile of spiritual maturity. The phrase "in the same way" (1 Pet 5:5) indicates a distinct group in a series. To wives and husbands (1 Pet 3:1,7), he adds younger persons. He urges those who are younger in the faith to submit to their elders, elders not only in age but more importantly in the faith. They join slaves, wives, and ordinary believers in their respect for the social order of the household of God.

Western culture's generational segregation leads to significant relational fragmentation and disorientation in the household of God. Peter never would have envisioned the church dividing along generational lines, but today it is common to divide along generational lines. This is not a fault of any particular generation, but the multigenerational nature of the household of God is a New Testament expectation. Younger believers are told to show "deference to authority" (1 Pet 5:5) and older believers are expected to show real humility.[1] Self-serving authority and self-centered autonomy are challenged by Peter's call for mutual humility.

ONE SIZE FITS ALL

Clothing was a useful metaphor in the ancient world because it was a universal indicator of social standing. It could be read faster than a resumé. The metaphor was popular with the apostles. Paul wrote, "Clothe yourselves with compassion, kindness, humility, gentleness, and patience" (Col 3:12). He challenged believers to "put on the full armor of God, so that you

---

1. Elliott, *1 Peter*, 841.

can take your stand against the devil's schemes" (Eph 6:10–11). Clothing defines roles. A uniform creates a set of expectations.

Peter simplified the clothing analogy, calling for everyone to wear the same garment, humility. Mutual humility was the uniform for the household of God, "a startling negation of the social distinctions" common in Roman antiquity.[2] The universal nature of the believer's clothing is especially telling as a follow-up to Peter's specific spiritual direction to subjects, slaves, wives, husbands, ordinary believers, elders, and younger persons. One size does fit all! Humility is for everyone regardless of their social standing, gender, age, and responsibility in the household of God.

Peter described the putting on of humility by using a unique verb that is used only here in the New Testament (ἐγκομβώσαθε). It is thought to refer to putting on "a garment or apron a slave tied over other garments in order to perform certain menial tasks."[3] The word for humility (ταπεινοφροσύνην) referred to "that way of thinking, feeling, and acting associated with the lowly."[4] In Greek society the word described "a lowly slave mentality, which is unworthy of the one who is free."[5] Everyone in the household of God was meant to share in this fundamental attitude toward one another. "All of you" (1 Pet 5:5) stresses the mutuality of such humility.[6]

Peter's words are different from the words used in John 13 to describe Jesus taking off his outer clothing and wrapping a towel around his waist, but the basic idea is the same. When Jesus deliberately dressed down, he dramatically portrayed his descent into humble service and sacrifice. Humility is a deliberate act of the will. Contrary to popular opinion, humility is not an unconscious act of good will. One of my professors used to say that the moment you thought you were humble you were guilty of pride. While this is a valid warning, it is better to emphasize that humility is a learned discipline of the will. Humility is not a natural gift nor a serendipitous feature of personality. Humility is an intentional commitment of the will in relationship to God and others. It is a chosen and cultivated quality of character that matures and deepens with the experience of Christ. Humility

---

2. Green, *1 Peter*, 170.
3. Achtemeier, *1 Peter*, 333.
4. Green, *1 Peter*, 170.
5. Goppelt, *A Commentary on 1 Peter*, 353.
6. Mutual humility is stressed in Paul's letters as well (Eph 4:2; 5:21; Phil 2:3; Col 3:12; Rom 12:10).

is the resolute self-emptying or surrender of the will to the commands of God and the needs of others.

Humility may be written off as a less-than-cool, churchy topic that decreases people's already shaky low self-esteem. "In this put-down world of ours, where we are browbeaten by bully bosses and thoughtless spouses," they protest, "don't talk about humility. We've had enough of gloomy piety, doormat theology, and self-demeaning put-downs. Give us hope, not humility!" We can empathize with people's concerns and share their criticism of false piety, but genuine, honest-to-goodness humility is not part of the problem; it is the solution. Humility before God is not the opposite of hope and grace, it is the foundation of God's blessing.

Jesus deliberately chose humility as an act of love. The Creator on bended knee humbly served the creature and the caption under John's picture reads, "He now showed them the full extent of his love." This unique act, divine foot-washing, is not out of character, but absolutely consistent with the divine love that serves and sustains us every single moment in all humility. The God who kneels is an apt description of God's saving grace.

> "If you have any encouragement from being united with Christ, if any comfort from his love, if any common sharing in the Spirit, if any tenderness and compassion, then make my joy complete by being like-minded, having the same love, being one in spirit and of one mind. Do nothing out of selfish ambition or vain conceit. Rather, in humility value others above yourselves, not looking to your own interests but each of you to the interests of the others. In your relationships with one another, have the same attitude of mind Christ Jesus had" (Phil 2:1–5).

When Jesus came to Peter on bended knee with towel and basin, Peter asked, "Lord, are you going to wash my feet?" (John 13:6). How did Peter ask this question, inquisitively or indignantly or in a tone somewhere in between? Jesus replied, "You do not realize now what I am doing, but later you will understand" (John 13:7). In the upper room the conflict between Jesus' humility and Peter's humiliation gets our attention. The Bible leads us to distinguish between humility and humiliation. They stand as opposites. Humility is a spiritual discipline rooted in the cross. It is an intentional commitment of the will in relationship to God and others. It is a chosen and cultivated quality of character that matures and deepens with our experience of Christ. Humility is a surrender of our will to the commands of God and the needs of others. The apostle's exhortation, "Have this mind in you which was also in Christ Jesus," calls for an intentional and resolute self-emptying (Phil 2:5).

Humility is the chosen awareness of our needy dependence on the mercy and wisdom of God. Humiliation is the feeling of shame, inadequacy, and disappointment that comes from our sinful self-reliance. Humiliation involves trusting in ourselves; humility involves trusting in God. Humiliation rejects God; humility bows before God. Humiliation leads to discouragement, disorientation, and despair; humility leads to hope. Humiliation thrives on self-promotion; humility frees us from the pressure to make a name for ourselves. Humiliation is our enemy, we feel it in our soul; but humility is our friend, whether we know it or not. For there is no other way to deal with humiliation than through humility.

The clash between humility and humiliation continues today in the defensive posture of the believer who clings to the ways of the world rather than the Jesus way. Jesus comes to us on his knees and, like Peter, we feel humiliated, disoriented, and upset. We don't understand the redemptive strategy that intends to turn our world upside down. We bargained for a saved soul, not a transformed life. When we came to Christ, we didn't count on Jesus' kingdom priorities. We thought "the first will be last and the last first" (Matt 20:16) was a nice slogan, not a reality that would change our world. We had no intention of making the poor and needy our priority, nor did we expect to reach out to the outcast and the outsider. We thought our goal was to climb the ladder of Christian success, but now we are learning that Jesus expects us to befriend the lonely and lost. First Peter is confirmation that Jesus' upper room message got through to Peter.

In typical fashion, Peter roots his spiritual direction in the Old Testament. There is a long tradition that roots maturity and holiness in humility. Peter quotes from Proverbs, "God opposes the proud but shows favor to the humble" (Prov 3:34). Peter reiterates his call to humility antiphonally. He answers his imperative call ("clothe yourselves with humility") with pastoral encouragement, "allow yourselves to be humbled," or accept your humble status (1 Pet 5:5–6).[7] Intentionality is combined with willed passivity. There is a combination here of conviction and compliance, determination and trust. There is no better place to be, no matter what the circumstances, than under God's mighty hand, who alone is worthy of all trust. Karen Jobes writes, "The command to be humbled under God's mighty hand is a command to accept, though not to seek, difficult circumstances as a part of

---

7. Elliott, *1 Peter*, 850.

Humility

God's deliverance, neither railing against God ('Why did this happen to me?' 'What did I do to deserve this?') nor raging against those causing the difficulty, but rather blessing those who insult and injure (1 Pet 3:9)."[8]

Humility is the precursor to exaltation. The "fellowship of Christ's sufferings" will give way to "the power of the resurrection" (Phil 3:10). Authentic faith will result "in praise, glory and honor when Jesus Christ is revealed" (1 Pet 1:7). Those who suffer for Christ will be "overjoyed when his glory is revealed" (1 Pet 4:13). They "will share in the glory to be revealed" (1 Pet 5:1) and will "receive the crown of glory that will never fade away" (1 Pet 5:4). As the psalmist said, "Those who sow in tears will reap with songs of joy" (Ps 126:5).

The proof of humility comes in the willingness to cast all our anxiety on God. If we trust in God, he will lift us up in due time. The *act* of humility is key to the *consequence* of peace. The two verses are inseparable and reflect Peter's synergistic aim of exhortation and encouragement.[9] Peter drew on Psalm 55:22: "Cast your cares on the Lord and he will sustain you; he will never let the righteous be shaken." Paul echoes the same conviction when he writes,

> Rejoice in the Lord always. I will say it again: Rejoice! Let your gentleness be evident to all. The Lord is near. Do not be anxious about anything, but in every situation, by prayer and petition, with thanksgiving, present your requests to God. And the peace of God, which transcends all understanding, will guard your hearts and your minds in Christ Jesus (Phil 4:4–7).

Sometimes you would think that believers are convinced that the most spiritual thing to do is worry over the future: the coming economic collapse, the moral crisis, the rise of secular humanism, and the reduction of American influence around the world. Peruse popular Christian books on Amazon and you may wonder if today's Christian is not driven more by fear than faith. In the Sermon on the Mount Jesus charged disciples not to worry. "I tell you, do not worry about your life, what you will eat or drink; or about your body, what you will wear" (Matt 6:25). What Jesus forbids is a "crippling anxiety that drives one to seek security by one's own efforts apart

---

8. Jobes, *1 Peter*, 312.

9. Elliott writes, "Our author brings the body of his letter to a close with another masterful blend of exhortation (5:5b, 6a, 7a, 8–9a) and encouragement (5:5c, 6b, 7b, 9b, 10–11), a combination exemplifying the twofold aim of the letter as a whole (5:12d)." Elliott, *1 Peter*, 868.

from the Father."[10] When we stop looking to our heavenly Father and start looking to ourselves, we fall into anxiety and worry. Even the basic necessities of life were meant to become the raw material for trusting in God.

The anxiety Peter has in mind is the worry generated by chronic and pervasive hostility directed against the messianic community. Peter gathers up *all* that anxiety and challenges believers to cast their care on the Lord, to trust in his sovereign and protective care.

RESIST THE DEVIL

Peter's plea for trust in the face of anxiety and adversity is followed by a challenge to remain vigilant. Like a good night watchman, believers are exhorted to stay awake and remain watchful (1 Pet 1:13; 4:7).[11] Throughout 1 Peter the focus has been on the faithfulness of the believer, not the badness of the world. No excuses are given to excuse disobedience. The apostles were reticent to make too much of the devil or blame the devil for Christians falling away.[12] James writes, "Submit yourselves to God. Resist the devil, and he will flee from you" (Jas 4:7). Peter affirms the dangerous reality of the devil (διάβολος) more for the purpose of warning Christians than excusing sinners. The devil is a slanderer who "prowls around like a lion looking for someone to devour" (1 Pet 5:8). The image of the ravenous lion in Psalm 22:13, a psalm focused on Christ's passion, may have been in Peter's mind.

Paul describes the devil as the ruler of the kingdom of the air, suggesting that the immediate inspiration for evil is as close and as penetrating as the air that we breathe. Like a cloud of pollution hanging over the city, the kingdom of the air reigns over his followers. His spirit "is now at work in those who are disobedient" (Eph 2:2). Evil's immediacy is like working in an office with thick secondhand smoke or living around radioactive material.

---

10. Guelich, *The Sermon on the Mount*, 336.

11. The word for "watchful" or "sober-minded" (γρηγορήσατε) is the same word used by Jesus in his Sermon on the end of the world (Matt 24:42; 25:13) and in the garden of Gethsemane (Matt 26:41).

12 In Hebrew, *Satan* means "adversary." Other titles include the devil, the Evil One, or the Tempter. Satan is a high angelic being who rebelled against God. Allusions to Satan may be found in Isaiah 14:12–14 and Ezekiel 28:11–16. Satan is called the "god of this age" and is blamed for blinding the minds of unbelievers (2 Cor 4:4). Jesus called him "the prince of this world" (John 14:30) and John said, "the whole world is under the control of the evil one" (1 John 5:19).

Danger pervades the atmosphere. In some cultures, there is a profound sense of the devil and the demonic inhabiting space, creating fear among those who sense the demonic presence. Yet the devil's inability to incarnate itself into the physical world is an indication of weakness. The demonic is limited to insinuation and is denied incarnation. The devil can infiltrate but the devil cannot embody. The "Word was made flesh" (John 1:14) but the devil remains disincarnate, incapable of assuming what he did not create. To preside over the "kingdom of the air" underscores this limitation and is indicative of the ethereal nature of the devil's being and work. Evil is the negative unreality of God's created good.

On the subject of the devil the Bible gives us enough information to be on guard, but not enough to indulge our curiosity. Markus Barth observes, "Though [the devil] is often mentioned in the Bible, it is impossible to derive an ontology, phenomenology, and history of Satan sufficiently complete to create a 'Satanology' which in the slightest measure corresponds to the weight of biblical 'theo-logy.'"[13] We were meant to be aware of the devil and the power of evil, but never engrossed in the subject. For example, no one need be a student of pornography to be on guard against pornography. To dwell on pornography would be to become its victim. Likewise with the devil, demonic power is real, but should not be fixated on. The spirit of the antichrist pervades the world but as John reminds us, "Greater is he that is in you than he that is in the world" (1 John 4:4).

Peter's brief description of the devil as a roaring lion is consistent with the Apostle John's description of the devil in Revelation 20. The power of the devil is held in check during the church age, metaphorically described as a millennium. For a symbolic thousand years the church will bear witness to the redemptive power of the Lamb. During that time "the dragon, that ancient serpent, who is the devil, or Satan," will be bound and kept from "deceiving the nations" (Rev 20:2).

This doesn't mean that the devil is literally in solitary confinement without influence or power. It is a figurative way of saying the devil's power is curtailed and limited. The Apostle John used the same word for binding Satan that Jesus used to describe the binding of the strong man (Matt 12:29). Satan's power was curtailed because of the presence of the incarnate one. Jesus said to his disciples, "I saw Satan fall like lightning from heaven" (Luke 10:17–18). "Now is the time for judgment on this world," Jesus said; "now the prince of this world will be driven out. But I, when I am lifted up

---

13. Barth, *Ephesians*, 228.

from the earth, will draw all men to myself" (John 12:31–32). The spirit of the antichrist pervades the world but as John reminds us, "Greater is he that is in you than he that is in the world" (1 John 4:4). The crucified and risen Lord has "disarmed the powers and authorities . . . triumphing over them by the cross" (Col 2:15).

The binding of Satan means that the church is free to "make disciples of all nations" (Matt 28:18–20). Satan's power is checked by the Spirit of Christ. Nevertheless, Peter warns, "Be alert and of sober mind. Your enemy the devil prowls around like a roaring lion looking for someone to devour. Resist him" (1 Pet 5:8–9).

Peter exhorts believers to resist the devil by "standing firm in the faith" (1 Pet 5:9). Believers are challenged to not only resist the ugly side of evil, but also the beautiful and seductive side of evil. Evil's hideous strength is not only fearsome and tyrannical, it is also thrilling and beautiful. There is a seductive side to evil that the inhabitants of the earth find attractive and compelling. The devil's influence is felt not only in violent acts of terrorism but in skyrocketing sales of pharmaceuticals and warheads. The oppressive world system legitimizes abortion on demand and turns children into immortality symbols. Evil is in the dark alley mugging and evil is in the corporate windfall. There is a bull market on Wall Street and poverty runs rampant. The streetwise pimp and the corporate CEO have something in common. The pervasiveness of evil and the universal sweep of idolatry fits the Apostle Peter's description of the devil on the prowl.

> Resistance to the Devil and firmness in faith include resistance to pressures urging conformity to a style of life that believers have renounced and resistance to the temptation to "go along in order to get along." Should Christians succumb to this pressure, they would indeed by "devoured" and absorbed by society at large, and this would have meant the end of the Christian movement in Asia Minor; hence the urgent need for vigilance, resistance, and firmness in faith.[14]

STAND FIRM, STAND FAST

Peter wrote his letter and Silas delivered it to the outposts of hope scattered throughout Asia Minor. His purpose was to encourage the "elect exiles"

---

14. Elliott, *1 Peter*, 860.

Humility

who were part of "the family of believers throughout the world" undergoing suffering for the sake of the gospel. Speaking as he has from the beginning, from an eschatological perspective, Peter made this promise: "And the God of all grace, who called you to his eternal glory in Christ, after you have suffered a little while, will himself restore you and make you strong, firm, and steadfast" (1 Pet 5:10).

Suffering is the letter's reoccurring theme; not state-sponsored violent persecution—that is yet to come—but the slander, abuse, and ridicule that Christians experience when they are redeemed "from the empty way of life handed down from [their] ancestors" (1 Pet 1:18). Instead of responding to verbal abuse and social ostracism with anger and resentment, Peter counsels submission. Let the pagans see your good deeds. "Do not repay evil with evil or insult with insult. . . . Do not fear their threats; do not be frightened" (1 Pet 3:9, 14). His bottom-up profile of spiritual maturity and ethical impact is illustrated by resilient slaves, faithful wives, and caring husbands, but inspired by Christ himself: "To this you were called, because Christ suffered for you, leaving you an example, that you should follow in his steps" (1 Pet 2:21).

Christ's suffering is central to the believer's identity in the household of God and it is strategic for the believer's social impact. There are eight specific references to the sufferings of Christ in 1 Peter. Christ's followers are chosen because of the obedience of Jesus and the sprinkling of his blood (1 Pet 1:2). The prophets longed to predict and understand "the sufferings of the Messiah," but now the good news of Christ's atoning sacrifice is preached to all by the Holy Spirit (1 Pet 1:11–12). Believers are redeemed "with the precious blood of Christ, a lamb without blemish or defect" (1 Pet 1:19) and called to serve according to Christ's sacrificial example (1 Pet 2:21). His atoning sacrifice is the basis for the believer's holiness. "He himself bore our sins in his body on the cross, so that we might die to sins and live for righteousness" (1 Pet 2:24). Disciples suffer for doing good, because "Christ also suffered once for sins, the righteous for the unrighteous, to bring you to God" (1 Pet 3:18). Their battle against sin is empowered and exemplified in Christ's suffering. "Therefore, since Christ suffered in his body, arm yourselves also with the same attitude . . ." (1 Pet 4:1). They rejoice "inasmuch as [they] participate in the sufferings of Christ" (1 Pet 4:13).

If we cannot find ourselves identified in this letter, encouraged by its teaching and exhorted by its challenge, we have to ask ourselves if we are seriously practicing New Testament Christianity. If we find 1 Peter irrelevant and foreign, it may be because we are practicing popular Christianity, not New Testament Christianity. Today we suffer from post-biblical Christianity, a version of Christianity that finds the New Testament strange and foreign. Peter saw it the other way around. The "elect exiles" were the ones who had become strange and foreign in their home cultures because of Christ.

The world leverages hate and fear; Christ's followers leverage love and faith. In every conflict, crisis, and challenge, we plant the cross and become like Jesus. First Peter challenges believers to stand firm and stand fast but not in a way envisioned by many Christian leaders today. The campaigns and crusades that leverage fear and resentment to call for a popular spiritual uprising to take back the nation and to conform culture to "Christian" principles ignore the Spirit-inspired Christ for culture strategy of 1 Peter. We are called to submission and sacrifice. Because Christ suffered, we suffer. Christ's followers are called to impress the pagan world with God's goodness: love instead of hate, purity instead of lust, fidelity instead of infidelity, honesty instead of dishonesty, reconciliation instead of retaliation, and prayer instead of revenge. Instead of being filled with resentment and anger, Christ's disciples are filled with hope and rejoicing. Christ left us his example and we follow in his steps.

> And the God of all grace, who called you to his eternal glory in Christ, after you have suffered a little while, will himself restore you and make you strong, firm and steadfast. To him be the power for ever and ever. Amen (1 Pet 5:10–11).

Bibliography

Achtemeier, Paul J. *1 Peter: A Commentary on First Peter*. Minneapolis: Fortress, 1996.
Barna, George. *Revolution: Finding Vibrant Faith Beyond the Walls of the Sanctuary*. Carol Stream, IL: Tyndale, 2006.
Barth, Karl. *Dogmatics in Outline*. New York: Harper, 1959.
Barth, Markus. *Ephesians*. The Anchor Bible, vol. 34. New York: Doubleday, 1974.
Baxter, Richard. *The Reformed Pastor*. Carlisle, PA: The Banner of Truth Trust, 2007.
Boring, M. Eugene. *1 Peter*. Abingdon New Testament Commentaries. Nashville: Abingdon, 1999.
Bonhoeffer, Dietrich. *The Cost of Discipleship*. New York: Macmillan, 1963.
Brown, Brené. "The Power of Vulnerability." TED.com, June 2010. https://www.ted.com/talks/brene_brown_on_vulnerability.
Bruner, Frederick Dale. *The Gospel of John*. Grand Rapids: Eerdmans, 2012.
———. *Matthew: A Commentary*. 2 vol. Grand Rapids: Eerdmans, 2004.
Bukowski, Charles. "The Laughing Heart." In *Betting on the Muse: Poems and Stories*, 400. New York: Harper Collins, 1996.
Calvin, John. *Hebrews and 1 and 2 Peter*. Grand Rapids: Eerdmans, 1994.
Carlson, Lois. *Monganga Paul*. New York: Harper & Row, 1966.
Carson, D. A. "1 Peter." In *Commentary on the New Testament Use of the Old Testament*, edited by G. K. Beale and D. A. Carson, 1015–45. Grand Rapids: Baker, 2007.
Chadwick, Henry. *Origen: Contra Celsum*. Cambridge: Cambridge University Press, 1953.
Chrysostom, John. "On the Priesthood." In *Nicene and Post-Nicene Fathers*, vol. 9, first series, edited by Philip Schaff, 25–83. Peabody, MA: Hendrickson, 1995.
———. "To Prove That No One Can Harm the Man Who Does Not Injure Himself." In *Nicene and Post-Nicene Fathers*, vol. 9, first series, edited by Philip Schaff, 267–84. Peabody, MA: Hendrickson, 1995.
Chambers, Oswald. *My Utmost for His Highest*. New York: Dodd, Mead & Company, 1935.
Clark, Chap. *Hurt: Inside the World of Today's Teenagers*. Grand Rapids: Baker, 2004.
Clowney, Edmund. *The Message of 1 Peter: The Way of the Cross*. Downers Grove, IL: InterVarsity, 1988.
Crouch, Andy. "Steve Jobs: The Secular Prophet." *The Wall Street Journal*, October 8, 2011.
Davids, Peter H. *The First Epistle of Peter*. Grand Rapids: Eerdmans, 1990.
Douthat, Ross. *Bad Religion: How We Became A Nation of Heretics*. New York: Free Press, 2012.
Dreyfus, Hubert, and Sean Dorrance Kelly. *All Things Shining: Reading the Western Classics to Find Meaning in a Secular Age*. New York: Free Press, 2011.

BIBLIOGRAPHY

Dryden, J. De Waal. *Theology and Ethics in 1 Peter: Paraenetic Strategies for Christian Character Formation*. Tübingen: Mohr Siebeck, 2006.

Dyrness, William A. "Aesthetics in the Old Testament: Beauty in Context." *Journal of the Evangelical Theological Society* 28/4 (December 1985) 421–32.

Elliott, John H. *A Home for the Homeless: A Social-Scientific Criticism of 1 Peter, Its Situation and Strategy*. Eugene, OR: Wipf & Stock, 2005.

———. *Conflict, Community, and Honor: 1 Peter in Social-Scientific Perspective*. Eugene, OR: Cascade, 2007.

———. *1 Peter: The Anchor Yale Bible*. New Haven, CT: Yale University Press, 2000.

Ellul, Jacques. *The Political Illusion*. New York: Vintage, 1972.

Fee, Gordon D. "The Priority of Spirit Gifting For Church Ministry." In *Discovering Biblical Equality*, edited by Ronald W. Pierce and Rebecca Merrill Groothius, 241–54. Downers Grove, IL: InterVarsity, 2004.

Gladwell, Malcolm. *David and Goliath: Underdogs, Misfits, and the Art of Battling Giants*. New York: Little, Brown and Company, 2013.

Gilbreath, Edward. *Reconciliation Blues: A Black Evangelical's Inside View of White Christianity*. Downers Grove, IL: InterVarsity, 2006.

Gillquist, Peter. "A Marathon We Are Meant to Win." *Christianity Today*, October 1981, 22–23.

Goppelt, Leonhard. *A Commentary on 1 Peter*. Translated by J. E. Alsup. Grand Rapids: Eerdmans, 1993.

Green, Joel B. *1 Peter: The Two Horizons New Testament Commentary*. Grand Rapids: Eerdmans, 2007.

Green, Michael. *Evangelism in the Early Church*. Grand Rapids: Eerdmans, 1975.

Greene, Joshua. *Moral Tribes: Emotion, Reason, and the Gap Between Us and Them*. New York: Penguin, 2013.

Grudem, Wayne. *1 Peter*. Tyndale New Testament Commentaries. Grand Rapids: Eerdmans, 1988.

Guelich, Robert A. *The Sermon on the Mount*. Waco, TX: Word, 1982.

Harink, Douglas. *1 & 2 Peter*. Brazos Theological Commentary on the Bible. Grand Rapids: Brazos, 2009.

Hart, David Bentley. "No Enduring City." *First Things*, August/September 2013, 45–51.

Hoffman, Shirl James. *The Good Game: Christianity and the Culture of Sports*. Waco, TX: Baylor University Press, 2010.

Horrell, David G. *1 Peter*. London: T & T Clark, 2008.

Horton, Michael S. "How the Kingdom Comes." *Christianity Today*, January 2006, 46.

Houston, James, and Bruce Waltke. *The Psalms as Christian Worship*. Grand Rapids: Eerdmans, 2010.

Hunter, George. *Radical Outreach: The Recovery of Apostolic Ministry and Evangelism*. Nashville: Abingdon, 2003.

Hunter, James Davison. *To Change The World: The Irony, Tragedy, and Possibility of Christianity in the Late Modern World*. New York: Oxford University Press, 2010.

Huxley, Aldous. *Brave New World*. London: Granada, 1977.

Isaacson, Walter. *Steve Jobs*. New York: Simon & Schuster, 2011.

ITV News. "Abortion activist defiant in death." September 22, 2003. www.itv.com/news/1763934.html.

James, Bruno. *Saint Bernard of Clairvaux*. New York: Harper, 1957.

Jobes, Karen H. *1 Peter*. Baker Exegetical Commentary on the New Testament. Grand Rapids: Baker, 2005.

Bibliography

Keller, Timothy. *Center Church: Doing Balanced, Gospel-Centered Ministry in Your City.* Grand Rapids: Zondervan, 2012.

———. *Counterfeit Gods: The Empty Promises of Money, Sex, and Power, and the Only Hope That Matters.* New York: Dutton, 2009.

Kierkegaard, Søren. *Attack Upon 'Christendom.'* Princeton, NJ: Princeton University Press, 1968.

———. *Works of Love.* New York: Harper & Row, 1962

Lewis, C. S. *The Weight of Glory.* New York: Collier, 1949.

Liefeld, Walter L. "The Nature of Authority in the New Testament." In *Discovering Biblical Equality*, edited by Ronald W. Pierce and Rebecca Merrill Groothius, 255–71. Downers Grove, IL: InterVarsity, 2004.

Lincoln, Andrew T. *Ephesians.* Word Biblical Commentary. Dallas: Word, 1990.

McCarthy, Cormac. *The Sunset Limited.* New York: Vintage, 2006.

McKnight, Scot. *1 Peter.* The NIV Application Commentary. Grand Rapids: Zondervan, 1996.

Michaels, J. R. *1 Peter.* Waco, TX: Word, 1988.

Mounce, Robert H. *Born Anew to a Living Hope: A Commentary on 1 and 2 Peter.* Grand Rapids: Eerdmans, 1982.

Mouw, Richard. "The Life of Bondage in the Light of Grace." *Christianity Today*, December 9, 1988, 41–42.

Newbigin, Lesslie. *The Gospel in a Pluralist Society.* Grand Rapids: Eerdmans, 1989.

Perkins, John. *A Quiet Revolution.* Waco, TX: Word, 1976.

Peterson, Eugene H. *The Message Remix.* Colorado Springs: NavPress, 2003.

———. *Reversed Thunder: The Revelation of John and the Praying Imagination.* San Francisco: Harper & Row, 1988.

Rushdie, Salman. Wikiquote. https://en.wikiquote.org/wiki/Salman_Rushdie.

Samuel, Vinay. "Religion: Cause or Cure for Terrorism? The Christian Church and a World of Religiously Inspired Violence." *SPU Response*, Spring 2003, 10.

Seaver, George. *David Livingstone: His Life and Letters.* New York: Harper & Brothers, 1957.

Snodgrass, Klyne. *Ephesians.* The NIV Application Commentary. Grand Rapids: Zondervan, 1996.

Stott, John R. W. *Christian Counter-Culture: The Message of the Sermon on the Mount.* Downers Grove, IL: InterVarsity, 1978.

Thielman, Frank. "First Peter: On Suffering as a Christian." In *The Theology of the New Testament*, 569–84. Grand Rapids: Zondervan, 2005.

Thiselton, Anthony C. *The First Epistle to the Corinthians.* The New International Greek Testament Commentary. Grand Rapids: Eerdmans, 2000.

Volf, Miroslav. *Captive to the Word of God: Engaging the Scriptures for Contemporary Theological Reflection.* Grand Rapids: Eerdmans, 2010.

Webb, Robert L., and Betsy Bauman-Martin, eds. *Reading First Peter With New Eyes: Methodological Reassessments of the Letter of First Peter.* London: T & T Clark, 2007.

White, R. E. O. "Salvation." In *The Evangelical Dictionary of Theology*, edited by Walter Elwell, 967–69. Grand Rapids: Baker, 1984.

Wright, N. T. *After You Believe: Why Christian Character Matters.* New York: HarperOne, 2010.

Yoder, John Howard. *The Politics of Jesus.* Grand Rapids: Eerdmans, 1972.

www.ingramcontent.com/pod-product-compliance
Lightning Source LLC
Chambersburg PA
CBHW031434150426
43191CB00006B/506